AF882128

Taxation in the Netherlands

Taxation in the Netherlands

FOURTH EDITION

Gerrit te Spenke

Updated by **Mark de Vries**

Wolters Kluwer
Law & Business

Published by:
Kluwer Law International
PO Box 316
2400 AH Alphen aan den Rijn
The Netherlands
Website: www.kluwerlaw.com

Sold and distributed in North, Central and South America by:
Aspen Publishers, Inc.
7201 McKinney Circle
Frederick, MD 21704
United States of America
Email: customer.service@aspenpublishers.com

Sold and distributed in all other countries by:
Turpin Distribution Services Ltd.
Stratton Business Park
Pegasus Drive, Biggleswade
Bedfordshire SG18 8TQ
United Kingdom
Email: kluwerlaw@turpin-distribution.com

Printed on acid-free paper.

ISBN 978-90-411-3167-6

© 2011 Kluwer Law International BV, The Netherlands

All rights reserved. No part of this publication may be reproduced, stored in a retrieval system, or transmitted in any form or by any means, electronic, mechanical, photocopying, recording, or otherwise, without written permission from the publisher.

Permission to use this content must be obtained from the copyright owner. Please apply to: Permissions Department, Wolters Kluwer Legal, 76 Ninth Avenue, 7th Floor, New York, NY 10011-5201, USA. Email: permissions@kluwerlaw.com

Printed in Great Britain.

About the Authors

Gerrit te Spenke studied tax law at Leiden University, where he graduated as Master in Tax Law in 1968. Until 1974 he worked for the Dutch Tax Authorities as a corporate tax inspector. In 1974, he joined the reputable tax law firm Meijburg & Co., which later became KPMG Meijburg & Co., where he became a partner until he resigned in 2007. Gerrit lives in Amsterdam where he is still active as a board member and supervisory board member of companies active in the music and Internet business. Moreover he is member of the board of several art foundations. Gerrit is the author of the first three editions of this book.

Mark J. de Vries studied notary law and civil law at the University of Groningen. He worked as a candidate notary public and solicitor before he became assistant professor at the University of Groningen in 1985. He wrote a thesis on the role of the civil judge in tax matters. He also works as a part time tax advisor for a big international tax firm. Mark updated the book for this fourth edition.

Table of Contents

List of Abbreviations

AAW	*Algemene Arbeidsongeschiktheidswet* (General Disablement Benefits Act)
AOW	*Algemene Ouderdomswet* (Old Age Pensions Act)
AWBZ	*Algemene Wet Bijzondere Ziektekosten* (Exceptional Medical Expenses Act)
AWW	*Algemene Weduwen -en Wezenwet* (General Widows' and Orphans' Benefits Act)
BTW	*Belasting op de Toegevoegde Waarde* (VAT)
BV	*Besloten Vennootschap* (Private Company)
CITA 69	Corporate Income Tax Act 1969
DWTA	(Dividend) Withholding Tax Act 1965
ECJ	European Court of Justice
ETA	Estate Tax Act 1956
EU	European Union
GAAL	General Act on Administrative Law
GATT	General Agreement on Tariffs and Trade
GTA	General Tax Act
IFRS	International Financial Reporting Standards
ITA	Income Tax Act 2001
OECD	Organisation for Economic Co-operation and Development
NV	*Naamloze Vennootschap* (Limited Liability Company)
SME	small to medium-sized enterprises
TFEU	Treaty on the Functioning of European Union
VAT	Value Added Tax
VATA	Value Added Tax Act

WAO	*Wet Arbeidsongeschiktheid* (Disablement Insurance Act)
WIR	*Wet Investerings Rekening* (Former Investment Premium)
WOZ	*Wet waardering onroerende zaken* (Real Estate Tax Act)
WW	*Werkloosheidswet* (Unemployment Insurance Act)
ZFW	*Ziekenfondswet* (Health Insurance Act)
ZW	*Ziektewet* (Sickness Benefits Act)

Preface

There has been a big gap between the third and fourth edition of this book. Therefore, I am very pleased that you finally see this new edition in front of you.

The importance of English-language information on the Netherlands tax system has grown due to the advancing internationalization. The aim of this book is to give foreign investors, company executives as well as lawyers, consultants and accountants a basic understanding of the Dutch tax system.

In the period between the two editions there have been many changes in Dutch taxation. For example, a new Income Tax Act, but also changes in almost all other fields of taxation. The book, which was originally written by Gerrit te Spenke, has been completely revised.

Several colleagues of the Tax Department of the University of Groningen have helped me with observations and criticisms. I would like to thank: Raymond Adema, Martin Boer, Jan Bouwman, Jan bij de Leij, Irene Burgers, Hans Halma and Nico Schutte.

M.J.d.V.
Groningen, May 2011

Chapter 1

General Introduction

1.1 THE TAX SYSTEM

The Netherlands tax system is based on a number of laws, some dating back many years. The right to levy a tax is based on the Constitution (*Grondwet*) which stipulates that taxes can only be levied if authorized by an Act of Parliament. Tax legislation is enacted in the same way as any other Act; that is, through cooperation of the Crown (Queen and Ministers) and Parliament (consisting of the First and Second Chamber). Both the Crown, in practice the Ministry of Finance, and the Second Chamber have the right to initiate bills, which must then be passed by both Chambers. Although most Dutch taxes are levied by the central government, local government authorities, too, may levy taxes indicated by law. The most important example is the real estate tax levied by municipalities.

The most important taxes are:

(a) income tax (see Chapter 3);
(b) corporate income tax (see Chapter 4);
(c) wages tax (see Chapter 5);
(d) (dividend) withholding tax (see Chapter 7);
(e) value added tax (see Chapter 8);
(f) estate and gift tax (see Chapter 9);
(g) tax on legal transactions (see Chapter 10);
(h) international (European) tax (see Chapter 11);
(i) miscellaneous, such as import duties and excise tax (see Chapter 12).

All these taxes are levied on the basis of various Acts; for example, the Income Tax Act of 2001, the Corporate Income Tax Act of 1969, etc.

There are, however, other Acts which also deal with taxation but which are of a more general nature. Examples are the Collection Act of 1990 (which replaced the Collection Act of 1845), the General Tax Act, the Customs Act and the Excise Act.

In this book only the General Tax Act, which applies to the so-called direct taxes, will be discussed in detail, as it contains a large number of rules regarding the application of direct taxes, assessments, objections, appeals, etc. (see Chapter 2).

1.2 COLLECTION OF TAXES

The collection of the taxes levied by the State, with the exception of customs and excise duties, is based on the Collection Act of 1990.

Collection is carried out by the collector of taxes. The time in which the various assessments must be paid depends on the kind of assessment.

Income tax and corporate income tax, whether provisional or final, must, in principle, be paid within two months after the date mentioned on the assessment. However, tax due on provisional assessments made in the year itself can be paid in the same number of instalments as there are months remaining in the year, unless the assessment is dated in October, November or December. In that case, the assessment should be paid within two months.

Additional ex officio income tax, corporate tax and net wealth tax assessments must be paid within one month after the date mentioned on the assessment.

Taxes not levied by assessment but through self-assessment must be paid when the return has to be filed. Additional ex officio assessments for these types of taxes must be paid within two weeks after the date of the assessment.

If a taxpayer fails to pay the tax within the statutory time limits he or she will receive a reminder shortly after the deadline for payment has passed. If he or she still fails to pay, the tax bailiff will serve a distress warrant and thereafter the assets of the taxpayer may be seized and sold. It should be noted in this respect that the tax collector can seize the assets of a taxpayer without a court order (which would be necessary under civil law).

If the only, or final, time limit for payment of an assessment has expired, the tax collector will charge interest at the statutory rate (which can differ quarterly) over the amount not yet paid.

In case of a reduction of an assessment, the tax collector will pay interest at the statutory rate over the amount of the reduction less the amount still due on the assessment. However, no interest will be paid if the assessment is reduced due to the carry back of losses or due to investment premiums.

The tax authorities have priority over other creditors but not priority over, for example, a mortgage.

The tax collector can also file a bankruptcy claim against a taxpayer (provided the requirements of the Bankruptcy Act are met).

1.3 TAX ADMINISTRATION

The taxes levied by the government are administered by *the Rijksbelastingdienst* (hereafter referred to as the revenue service). The revenue service falls within the jurisdiction of the Ministry of Finance. The Minister and the Under Minister of Finance (*staatssecretaris*) bear the political responsibility. The Ministry of Finance issues both published and unpublished directives regarding the interpretation of the laws, which as such do not have the force of law but are as a rule followed by the tax administration.

Once published, the taxpayer can request the application of these directives. If the directives are not applied by the tax inspector, the taxpayer can ask the tax courts to have the directives applied. The tax courts can interpret the directives. The taxpayer can appeal a tax court's decision regarding the application and/or interpretation of a directive to the Supreme Court.

Chapter 2
The General Tax Act

2.1 GENERAL PRINCIPLES

The General Tax Act (*Algemene wet inzake rijksbelastingen* of 2 July 1959), referred to as GTA, contains rules which apply to the imposition of all taxes levied by the State. Since 1992, the General Act on Administrative Law (*Algemene wet bestuursrecht*), referred to as GAAL, also applies partly to the taxes levied in the Netherlands. The various taxes to which the GTA applies did not come into force on the same date.

The provisions of the GTA do not apply automatically to taxes not levied by the State, but only by express appointment.

2.1.1 Definitions

The law contains several definitions ('tax law', 'tax inspector', 'tax court', etc.). Article 2 defines 'the Kingdom' as the Netherlands. Consequently, for tax purposes, Curaçao, St Maarten and Aruba are not a part of 'the Kingdom'. 'The Netherlands' is defined as the part of the kingdom situated in Europe. According to Article 1.1, the GTA applies only to 'the Netherlands'.

As of 1 January 1990, for application of the income tax, the wages tax, the corporate income tax and the insurance tax, the Netherlands part of the continental shelf (the sea-bed with its subterranean area outside the territorial waters, as far as the Netherlands is authorized to exercise exploitation rights on the basis of international law) is held to be a part of 'the Netherlands'.

2.1.2 Residence

The GTA (Article 4) provides that residence of an individual or a legal entity for tax purposes is determined 'according to the circumstances'. Some tax laws, however, contain an exception to this rule. According to Article 2, paragraph 4, of the Corporate Income Tax Act 1969, also referred to as CITA 69, a corporation or other legal entity incorporated under Netherlands law is deemed to be a resident of the Netherlands, with a few exceptions. For dividend withholding tax the same rule applies.

2.1.3 Contents of the GTA

Apart from an introduction (Chapter I), the GTA contains provisions on the following subjects:

- tax returns (section 2.2);
- taxes levied by assessment (section 2.3);
- self-assessment taxes (section 2.4);
- objection and appeal (section 2.6);
- interest (section 2.7);
- anti-avoidance procedure (section 2.8);
- international tax matters (section 2.9);
- special subjects; representation, supply of information to the tax authorities (section 2.10);
- administrative fines;(section 2.5)
- offences, penalties (section 2.5);
- Special Provisions (section 2.10).

2.2 TAX RETURN

2.2.1 When to File?

The tax inspector issues a tax return form to a person who, in his or her opinion, is liable to the relevant tax. Paper forms are hardly used nowadays. Tax returns are normally filed by internet and in many cases filled in online. When a digital tax return is requested by the tax authorities, the inspector issues an ‘invitation to file a tax return’ instead of issuing a form.

The taxpayer is obliged to file the completed return with the tax inspector. Not to file is a criminal offence. If the person receiving a form is not taxable for the tax concerned, he or she may, of course, indicate so in the return.

If a taxpayer does not receive a form or an invitation to file a tax return, he or she is obliged to ask for one (Article 6.3 GTA and Articles 2 and 3 Implementing Regulations (*Uitvoeringsregeling*) for the GTA).

- with respect to taxes based on assessments: within six and a half months after expiration of the taxation period (usually a calendar year);
- with respect to inheritance tax: within eight and a half months after the decease;

- with respect to gift tax: within two and a half months after the end of the year in which the donation took place;
- with respect to self-assessment taxes: before the date on which the tax is to be paid.

2.2.2 Time of Filing

Tax returns for taxes levied by assessment have to be filed within the period determined by the tax inspector, with a minimum of one month. The tax inspector can, at the request of the taxpayer, extend that period. The tax inspector may, when extending the period, require that a provisional return be filed.

If the return is not filed within the (extended) period, the tax inspector will remind the taxpayer by letter that no return has been filed. If the return is not filed within the period indicated in that letter (usually 10 days), the taxpayer can be fined. This fine is a fixed amount, that can however vary according to the frequency of non-returns in the recent past. For taxes levied by assessment and wage tax, the fine will be maximum Euro (EUR) 4,920 (2011), for other self-assessment taxes the maximum fine will be EUR 1,230 (2011).

For self-assessment taxes the return also has to be filed within a period of at least one month after having been issued. Usually the period ends on the date the tax is to be paid (see section 2.4.1). Extension may be granted subject to conditions made by the tax inspector.

2.3 TAXES LEVIED BY ASSESSMENT

The main taxes levied by assessment are:

- personal income tax;
- corporate income tax;
- gift tax and inheritance tax.

2.3.1 Assessment

For (corporate) income tax, the tax inspector makes out the assessment after having received the tax return.

The tax inspector can make out a provisional assessment.

The first provisional assessment is usually made in February of the relevant tax year itself and is based on the last known taxable income. A second provisional assessment can be made after the granting of an extension for filing the tax return.

Provisional assessments may be reduced if supported by a reasoned and documented request (objection).

The final assessment follows after examination of the tax return by the tax office. This also applies to gift tax and inheritance tax. If no tax return has been filed, the tax inspector may issue a final assessment based on a reasonable estimate of the taxpayer's income (taxable profit). The declarations for corporate and income tax for domestic taxpayers have to be done by electronic means. The assessments still are on paper.

2.3.2 Failure to Issue a Final Assessment

The tax inspector has to make out a final assessment within three years after the end of the (financial) year. The three-year period is, however, extended by the period of extension granted for filing the return.

If no assessment has been issued within the prescribed period the taxpayer cannot be assessed for that year. The Supreme Court has ruled that in such a case the provisional assessments should be refunded. The wages tax and the dividend withholding tax withheld will only be refunded insofar as they exceed the income tax which would have been due if an assessment could have been issued.

2.3.3 Additional Assessment, Statute of Limitations

If it appears that no tax or too little tax has been levied for a certain year, the tax inspector may issue an additional assessment. However, such an assessment can only be issued:

(a) Within a period of five years after the end of the (financial) year. (If in case of a carry back of losses the amount of the losses taken into account was too high, the additional assessment can be issued within five years after the end of the financial year in which the losses originated.) The extensions referred to in section 2.3.2 apply accordingly. As of 8 June 1991, the five-year term has been extended to twelve years with respect to foreign net wealth and income items.

(b) If there appear to be 'new facts' or circumstances of which the tax inspector was not aware and could not reasonably have been aware of at the time of the final assessment. This latter condition does not apply in a case where too high an amount of wages tax and/or dividend withholding tax has been deducted. The doctrine of the 'new fact' has been developed by the Supreme Court in a large number of decisions. These decisions can be briefly summarized as follows:

   (i) An additional assessment cannot be based on a change in the opinion of the tax inspector, even if a new (Supreme) court decision has been published after the date of the final assessment.

   (ii) If facts were not taken into account when the final assessment was issued, but should have been taken into account because the tax inspector was or could have been aware of them, such facts do not justify an additional assessment. For example: facts mentioned in the tax return or correspondence with the tax office; facts discovered by or mentioned to the tax auditor but not reported to the tax inspector; facts of which the tax inspector should have been aware because they are common knowledge (e.g., general trends in prices of real estate).

(iii) The doctrine of the 'new fact' has been developed because the taxpayer should be able to trust that the final assessment will not be followed by an additional assessment. Consequently, an additional assessment is possible where a mistake in the final assessment (although resulting from a mistake at the tax office) is evident to the taxpayer (e.g., an assessment on an income of EUR 10,000 instead of EUR 100,000). Although there is no 'new fact' in such a case an additional assessment may be issued.

As of 1 May 1994, the application of the 'new fact doctrine' has been limited to situations where the taxpayer acted in good faith. The taxpayer who on purpose does not give all the necessary information to the tax inspector for a correct assessment, never acts in good faith. The tax inspector has to prove bad faith.

As of 1 January 2010, additional assessment is possible in all cases where the taxpayer did know or could be supposed to know, that no tax or too little tax had been levied because of an error made by the tax authorities. The doctrine of 'new fact' has lost much of its importance by this measure.

2.4 TAXES LEVIED BY SELF-ASSESSMENT

The major taxes levied by self-assessment are:

- wages tax;
- turnover tax (VAT);
- dividend withholding tax.

Other taxes (road tax, real estate transfer tax, capital tax, insurance tax, lottery tax, etc.) are also levied by self-assessment. The provisions of the GTA apply to these taxes. In this chapter, however, specific provisions regarding the latter taxes will not be discussed.

2.4.1 RETURN AND PAYMENT

The taxpayer must pay within a month after the end of the period to which the tax applies and file a return after one month, at least, after receiving the invitation for declaration. The period for which the tax has to be paid is a calendar quarter, unless the tax inspector decides that the tax has to be paid monthly, or the taxpayer prefers monthly payments. In special cases the tax inspector can agree to annual returns. Wages tax is paid monthly.

If VAT has to be paid quarterly, the tax inspector may require that the taxpayer pay estimated amounts in the second and third month of the quarter. These payments are deducted in the quarterly return.

2.4.2 Assessment, Statute of Limitations

If no tax has been paid or it has not been fully paid (or an excess refund is granted, for example, for VAT), the tax inspector may levy the difference by way of assessment. For such an assessment no 'new fact' (see section 2.3.3) is required, since the tax inspector is normally not in a position to examine the quarterly or monthly returns.

No assessment is possible at a date later than five years after the end of the calendar year in which the tax liability arose or the refund was granted. Thus, the wages tax for the year 2003 cannot be assessed after 31 December 2008. A refund of VAT on, for example, 15 February 2004 cannot be reclaimed by an assessment later than 31 December 2009.

2.5 ADMINISTRATIVE PENALTIES

The GTA and the GAAL both contain provisions regarding administrative fines. The GAAL gives the formal rules by which the fines are applied, the GTA gives the circumstances under which an administrative tax fine can be imposed. The latter defines the punishable offences.

A distinction has to be made in the GAAL and the GTA between a punitive fine and a default surcharge. For default surcharges (*verzuimboetes*) it is not necessary to have deliberate intent or gross negligence. For a punitive fine one of these elements is necessary.

2.5.1 Punitive Fines

The maximum amount of the punitive fine can be 100%, and in some cases even 300% of the extra tax levied. This tax can be levied either by means of an additional assessment or by correcting the incorrect tax return filed by the taxpayer and imposing a higher first assessment. The maximum rates apply only if serious fraud by the taxpayer has caused the original assessment to be too low (or caused the fact that the tax inspector decided not to issue an assessment). A maximum fine of 50% may be imposed if the additional assessment was caused by the taxpayer's deliberate intent or of 25% if the additional assessment was caused by his or her gross negligence. There are similar fines for intentional default of payment of self-assessment taxes.

In practice a penalty of 100%, and sometimes even up to 300%, is the exception. According to written guidance of the Ministry of Finance, the tax inspector usually issues a penalty of 25% or 50% of the additional tax. The tax courts are not bound by the Ministry guidance and they can reduce the penalty even further.

A penalty of 100% – 300% is only levied in case of serious or repeated fraud. In addition, it follows from several court decisions that no penalty may be imposed if the taxpayer (although having been negligent) cannot be accused of serious negligence, which is close to fraudulent intent. In the case of simple omissions no punitive fine may therefore be imposed.

If a taxpayer voluntarily provides the correct information within two years after an incorrect tax declaration was made, there will not follow any kind of punishment. This is called the voluntary disclosure. If the two-year period is exceeded, the amount of the fine imposed will be largely reduced.

No administrative penalty applies if the taxpayer is convicted by a criminal court of an offence described in Article 68 or 69 GTA (intentional or unintentional filing of a false return, not filing a return, giving false information, etc.). Thus, a combination of the administrative penalty and a conviction by the regular court – fine or imprisonment – is not possible. The administrative penalty is also cancelled if a taxpayer is acquitted in respect of a criminal charge. Thus, the authorities must, in fact, make their choice between imposing an administrative penalty and formally accusing the taxpayer of one of the above offences at an early stage. Apart from very serious cases in the vast majority of cases the administrative penalty is imposed. (For objection, see section 2.6.1.)

The so-called *Vierde tranche* or fourth slice, of the GAAL was introduced in July 2009 with, among other objectives, the intention to be able to fine third parties. Forms of participation in an offence like being a co-perpetrator giving orders or actually having control of a prohibited conduct which are elements of the general criminal law now also have found a place in administrative law. For punitive fines (*vergrijpboetes*) co-perpetrators can now also be administratively fined. A tax advisor, for example, can be subjected to the general criminal law as a co-perpetrator. Now, a tax advisor who in cooperation with the tax payer files an incorrect tax return can himself or herself be fined.

If the co-perpetrator of a punitive fine has gross negligence he or she can be fined 25% of the assessment. If the co-perpetrator had deliberate intent the fine can even be 50% of the assessment.

2.5.2 Default Surcharges

In the case of taxes that are levied by self-assessment, the tax levied by an assessment referred to in section 2.4.2 can also be accompanied by an administrative fine of 100% of the amount levied (in practice the penalty varies from 0% to 100%, depending on the degree of guilt or negligence of the taxpayer).

Where the fact that the tax paid is too low is not the result of fraud or gross negligence on the part of the taxpayer, the default surcharge is restricted to 10% of the tax due, according to the provisions of the GTA. Thus (contrary to the rules for additional assessments described above), a penalty is even levied where the taxpayer unintentionally paid too little tax or paid the tax after the due date. In principle the surcharge will be 2% of the tax overdue, the maximum penalty is EUR 4,920. There are instances where the surcharge is imposed without an assessment accompanying it. This is the case when a payment is made too late, but before an assessment has been issued.

2.5.3 Administrative Fines in Tax Collection

In the collection of taxes the same system as described above applies. Both administrative fines and criminal penalties can be applied, but they may not regard the same offence. Non-payment of taxes, or payment after the period granted by law, can be punished by imposing an administrative fine.

The Collection of State Taxes Act 1990 (*Invorderingswet* 1990) mentions as examples of criminal offences, among. other things the not, unjust or incomplete providing of obligatory information. The providing of false information or not providing a proof of identity, or not allowing to have copies of necessary information made, are criminal offences also.

2.5.4 Administrative Fines and Human Rights

According to the Supreme Court, the levying of the administrative penalty is a criminal charge as meant in Article 6 of the Convention for the Protection of Human Rights and Fundamental Freedoms (Rome, 1950) and therefore the provisions of the third paragraph of that article should be observed by the tax authorities. For example, if the taxpayer has not been informed in writing of the reason why an administrative penalty is imposed at the time he or she receives the decision to impose the administrative penalty, the penalty has to be withdrawn. According to the principle of *praesumptio innocentiae*, the burden of proof of gross negligence and of deliberate intent rests on the tax authorities.

2.6 OBJECTION AND APPEAL

2.6.1 Objections

Objections can be lodged against:

- all assessments except provisional assessments, these will be reduced on request (see section 2.3.3);
- all administrative fines;
- decisions by the tax inspector by determination letter (*voor bezwaar vatbare beschikking*) not to levy a tax by assessment – an objection may be in the

taxpayer's interest if the wages tax and/or dividends tax are higher than the total income tax;
- any other decision by the tax inspector based on any relevant tax Act, provided such decision is given by determination letter. The taxpayer can also object against decisions based on treaties entered into by the Netherlands (for example. a refusal to grant a refund of dividend withholding tax), provided that the decree for ratifying the treaty provides (as is usual) that the tax inspector has to decide upon a request by determination letter;
- against a tax paid according to a return filed by the taxpayer himself or herself, or against a tax withheld from a person (e.g., an employee who feels that the wages tax withheld by the employer was too high).

No objections can be lodged against decisions of the tax inspector for which the form of a determination letter is not prescribed.

2.6.2 Decision by the Tax Inspector

The decision by the tax inspector upon an objection filed by the taxpayer is given by a formal decision in writing (*uitspraak*) in which the tax inspector has to explain the reasons of his or her decision. As of 1 January 1994, the law requires the tax inspector to make a formal decision within six weeks after the objection has been filed. This period can be extended by another four weeks, or more if the taxpayer agrees with that extension.

If the inspector does not issue the formal decision within this period, the taxpayer can file an appeal with the tax court (see section 2.5.3).

The tax inspector may require the taxpayer to provide additional information. Conversely, the taxpayer may request a meeting with the tax inspector before the latter issues his or her formal decision. A refusal by the tax inspector to meet with the taxpayer does not, however, provide grounds for an appeal.

2.6.3 Appeal

The taxpayer may file an appeal with the tax court against all formal decisions of the tax inspector referred to under section 2.5.1 and against the failure of the tax inspector to give a formal decision within the period prescribed by the law (see section 2.5.2).

The appeal has to be filed within six weeks after the date of the tax inspector's formal decision. The appeal should contain a description of the issue and a summary of the grounds for appeal, so that it is clear to the court how high, in the taxpayer's opinion, the tax should be.

N.B. The court procedure is, for the major part, not regulated in the GTA, but in the GAAL.

With the consent of the tax inspector, the taxpayer can file an appeal with the tax court rather than file an objection in the cases referred to in section 2.5.1. This is useful if the taxpayer and the tax inspector want a court decision on a specific question of law as quickly as possible.

2.6.4 Burden of Proof on the Taxpayer

Generally speaking the court is free to assign the burden of proof. If, however, the taxpayer (1) refuses to answer questions from a tax inspector; or (2) to supply information to the tax inspector where he or she has a legal obligation to give that information; or (3) did not file a proper return, although he or she was legally obliged to do so, the burden of proof is on the taxpayer to show that the assessment or decision of the tax inspector is incorrect.

2.7 INTEREST

As of 1 April 1987, Chapter VA was introduced in the GTA.

Chapter VA contains provisions regarding the assessment and payment of interest by the tax inspector (not to be confused with the charging and reimbursing of interest by the tax collector; *see* section 1.2).

2.7.1 Payment of Interest

Interest has to be refunded by the tax office if too much tax has been paid, and it will be charged by the tax office if too little tax is paid.

2.7.2 Charging of Interest

The tax office will charge interest of the taxpayer or the person liable to deduct and transfer wage tax. The percentage of the interest can differ quarterly. The tax collector determines the amount; he or she has the power of disposition. Interest will not be charged if the additional assessment is imposed after a voluntary improvement of an assessment done within three months after the end of the calendar year or the financial year of the tax involved.

(There is also a so-called revision interest, for which we refer to the GTA, Article 30i.)

2.8 ANTI-AVOIDANCE PROVISIONS

The tax inspector may decide to ignore for tax purposes certain transactions entered into by the taxpayer, if he or she can prove (e.g., because these transactions did not materially affect the economic situation of the taxpayer) that such transactions would not have been concluded if they would not have been expected to result in avoidance or reduction of direct taxes.

The tax inspector can apply the abuse of law doctrine (*fraus legis*), which is based on case law, according to which the intent and purpose of the tax law should prevail over the transactions entered into by the taxpayer. It gives the judge the possibility to eliminate or substitute certain transactions so that tax can be levied.

If the taxpayer uses certain tax efficient arrangements to avoid the levying of tax and the motive for using these is just avoiding paying tax, there will be *fraus legis*. If the taxpayer can prove or displace the assumption that it was not his or her sole or primary intention to avoid tax paying and if he or she has a good reason for the arrangement used, *fraus legis* will not be applied.

2.9 INTERNATIONAL MATTERS

Chapter VII of the GTA authorizes the government or the Minister of Finance to provide for unilateral, bilateral and multilateral arrangements for the avoidance of double taxation. Several decrees are based on this authorization. The more important are:

- the Unilateral Decree for the Avoidance of Double Taxation (providing for exemption of certain income from foreign sources of resident taxpayers, etc.);
- the Decree of the Minister of Finance regarding Exemption of Diplomatic and Consular Officials of Other Nations;
- bilateral tax Conventions and multilateral Conventions which contain provisions for relief from double taxation and which require the approval of Parliament.

The contents of the decrees and treaties are not discussed in this chapter (see sections 3.13, 4.13 and Chapter 11).

2.10 SPECIAL PROVISIONS

2.10.1 Representation

The taxpayer can appoint a representative. The tax inspector may, however, require that the taxpayer accompany his or her representative if he or she wishes the taxpayer to answer certain questions. The tax inspector may refuse representation by a specific person for valid reasons. He or she may also, for valid reasons, refuse representation if the taxpayer is in a position to meet his or her obligations (e.g., to answer specific questions) himself or herself. (This will not often happen if the taxpayer appoints a professional adviser, for example a tax adviser, auditor or lawyer.) (See sections 2.3.4 and 2.4.3 for the liability of these tax advisors.)

The law further contains rules regarding the representation of legal entities and minors and regarding persons who can act after the death of a taxpayer.

2.10.2 Obligations of the Taxpayers

2.10.2.1 General

Obviously, the taxpayer is obliged to provide the tax inspector with the necessary information regarding his or her own matters; that is, submit documents which may affect his or her tax liabilities, to allow the tax officials to check his or her records, answer questions regarding tax matters, etc.

Employers have the same obligations in respect of payroll tax.

Persons who carry on a business or liberal profession and all legal entities also have the obligation to submit to the tax inspectors accounts and documents and to supply all information which may be important for the determination of the tax liability of third parties.

These obligations regard all information that may possibly be of interest for the determination of the tax liabilities of the taxpayer concerned. No direct connection with, for example, financial records is required.

The law provides that clergymen, lawyers, notaries, pharmacists and members of medical professions can refuse information on the basis of their professional secrecy rules. Auditors and tax advisers have no legal rights to refuse information concerning their clients; however, the Ministry of Finance has ruled that the tax authorities may not demand that auditors and tax advisors submit their correspondence with clients, or supply information about their clients when these advisors do not wish to do so.

2.10.2.2 Supply of Information in International Relations

On 5 March 1991, the Netherlands Parliament accepted a bill which extends the duty to supply information in international relations. The bill entered into force on 21 March 1991.

According to the bill, the tax inspector is entitled to request from taxpayers information and (copies of) books and records held by a non-resident individual who or by a non-resident entity which directly or indirectly holds an interest of more than 50% in the taxpayer.

This also applies with respect to a non-resident individual or a non-resident entity which holds an interest of less than 50%, provided he or she, together with other individual(s) or entity/entities based on a mutual agreement to cooperate, holds an interest of more than 50%. The term 'mutual agreement to cooperate' is not defined. In the parliamentary records, reference was made to joint-venture agreements.

The inspector is also entitled to ask the taxpayer for information and (copies of) books and records from foreign sister companies. A company is defined as a sister company if a foreign individual or a foreign company directly or indirectly holds an interest of more than 50% in both the taxpayer and the foreign company.

The information requested has to be of relevance for the determination of the taxable income of the taxpayer.

Failure to comply with a request of the tax inspector will cause the burden of proof to be fully shifted to the taxpayer. This means that the tax inspector is free in establishing the taxable income and the taxpayer has to prove that the taxable income as established by the tax inspector is too high.

Furthermore, the failure to comply, whether intentional or unintentional, is considered to be an offence. The maximum penalties are:

- four years imprisonment; and/or
- a fine according to the Penal's Code maximum for this penalty or, if higher, 100% of the tax which the taxpayer tried to evade.

The above in principle also applies if foreign legislation forbids the foreign entity to give the requested information to the taxpayer.

However, in such a case it is up to the tax courts to decide whether or not, as a consequence of the failure to supply the information, the burden of proof should be shifted to the taxpayer.

Furthermore, in such a case (or if the foreign shareholder or sister company refuses to give the information and the taxpayer cannot be blamed for such a refusal), the failure to supply the information is not considered to be an offence.

The duty to supply information in first instance does not exist if the foreign shareholder or the foreign sister company is a resident of:

(a) a country which is a member of the European Union (EU);
(b) Curaçao, St Maarten and Aruba;
(c) a country with which the Netherlands has concluded a tax treaty, provided the treaty contains a provision for the exchange of information.

The reason underlying this provision is that the Netherlands can ask for the relevant information directly from the competent authorities of those countries.

Most tax treaties nowadays do contain a provision for the exchange of information. However, if the relevant information cannot be obtained via such an exchange of information, then the tax inspector, after having received permission from the Ministry of Finance, can follow the procedure described above, and ask the taxpayer to provide the relevant information.

2.10.3 Domicile

A non-resident taxpayer who files an objection, request or appeal must indicate an address (domicile) within the Netherlands.

2.10.4 Extension of Period for Objection and Appeal

Where an objection or appeal is filed too late, the objection or appeal will be dismissed, unless it can reasonably be held that this failure was not due to the neglect of the taxpayer.

2.10.5 Confidential Treatment of Information

According to Article 67 GTA, tax officials, etc., may not publish or pass on any information regarding persons or their affairs obtained in the execution of their duties, except insofar as this is necessary to levy or collect the tax. Thus, a tax inspector may inform his or her colleagues, the tax auditor, the tax collector, but not other government bodies. The Minister of Finance may, however, release the tax officials from this obligation. On the basis of this authority the minister has allowed tax offices to give information to other (semi-) governmental bodies and private institutions (e.g., the social security authorities, communities who support individuals, schools which levy school fees depending on income, etc.).

The Ministry of Finance observes this principle by not answering questions submitted by members of Parliament relating to individual persons or legal entities.

2.11 OFFENCES, PENALTIES

Chapters VIIIA and IX contain administrative and penal provisions (e.g., filing a false return, providing incorrect information to the tax authorities, or not answering questions put by the tax authorities).

With respect to intentional acts or omissions, the law provides for imprisonment (maximum six years in some cases) and fine (maximum EUR 4,920, 2011) or, if higher, 100% of the tax deliberately not paid. No proceedings are started if the taxpayer voluntarily files an amended return or adjusts the false information before he or she knows or may assume that the tax authorities are aware of the fact that the return (information) was incorrect.

Chapter 3
Income Tax

3.1 GENERAL

3.1.1 General Principles

The income tax provided for in the Income Tax Act of 2001 (ITA 2001) is levied on individuals at partly progressive and partly fixed rates.

These income can come from different sources; the income tax distinguishes three categories, which are known as 'boxes'. The total of the tax owed in these three boxes is the income tax payable.

The tax is levied by the State. There is no such tax levied by lower bodies such as municipalities. The basis for the calculation of the tax is the taxable income as calculated in the annual return, which must be filed before 1 April of the year following the tax year, unless an extension has been granted. An extension for filing can be automatically granted until 1 July of that year, provided an estimate of the income for that concerning year is filed. Professionals can file returns for their clients and generally obtain a further extension under certain conditions.

Taxpayers are either resident individuals or non-resident individuals. Nationality is irrelevant, but may be a factor in deciding residence. A definition of residence is provided for in the GTA (*Algemene Wet Rijksbelastingen*). Article 4 of that act states that residence must be determined according to the circumstances. In this respect a number of facts may be of relevance, such as whether the taxpayer keeps (permanent) personal ties with the Netherlands; whether the individual has a house available in the Netherlands; where his or her family lives; registration in a municipal register, etc. A resident taxpayer leaving the Netherlands but returning within one year will be deemed resident during that period, unless he or she establishes residence (according to the Netherlands rules) in another country. Netherlands diplomats and other civil servants, including their families, are deemed to remain residents of the Netherlands during their assignment abroad.

Foreign diplomats as well as representatives of certain international institutions are, on the other hand, exempted from Netherlands income tax. Resident taxpayers are subject to the tax on their worldwide income derived within a calendar year. Worldwide income is the total of the income derived from the various sources, less the expenses in connection therewith.

This income may be further decreased by certain deductible items which are not directly related to a specific source of income.

Resident taxpayers are in principle subject to income tax on their worldwide income or profits. Non-resident taxpayers are only liable to Netherlands income tax for income derived from a limited number of domestic sources. To protect resident taxpayers from double taxation which may result from the worldwide income principle, the Netherlands has concluded a large number of double taxation treaties. If no treaty applies, double tax relief may be obtained on the basis of the Unilateral Decree. For certain foreigners who are temporarily assigned to the Netherlands by a foreign employer, special rules may apply. These rules can be found in the Wage Tax Act.

3.1.2 Married Couples and Minor Children

In principle every taxpayer will only be taxed on his or her own income. There are, however, some exceptions: certain income in Box 3 of a partner (provided both partners are residents of the Netherlands) – unless separated – and certain income of minor children must be added.

3.1.2.1 Partners

Partners will be taxed separately on income in box 1:

(a) profits from an enterprise;
(b) net income from employment and other activities not qualifying as profit or employment income, as well as certain social security payments; or any other income subject to wages tax;
(c) a limited part of the profit of the enterprise carried on by the partner, in relation to the time spent by the spouse on behalf of that enterprise;
(d) periodic payments, including life annuities.

From this income the following items can be deducted:

(a) increases – less decreases – of the old age reserve;
(b) the allowance for self-employment (*zelfstandigenaftrek*);
(c) the cooperation allowance (*meewerkaftrek*, a deduction from business profit of an individual in case his or her partner is also working in the business);
(d) premiums in respect of periodic payments;
(e) small to medium-sized enterprises (SME) profit exemption (*MKB winstvrijstelling*).

3.1.2.2 Minor Children

Minor children are taxed separately on:

(a) profits from an enterprise;
(b) profits from a substantial interest;
(c) net income from employment and other activities.

The Box 3 income of minor children as well as their personal liabilities will always be included in the Box 3 income of the parents. See for tariffs Appendix I.

3.2 DEFINITION OF INCOME

3.2.1 General

The ITA defines 'income' as the aggregate income from the three boxes.

These three boxes, each with their own rate, are.:

– Box 1, taxable income from work and dwelling;
– Box 2, taxable income from substantial interest;
– Box 3, taxable income from savings and investments.

3.2.2 Computation

Different rules apply to each separate source of income in Box 1 for the computation of the income derived from that source. It is important to determine from which source the income was derived. The law lays down a specific order. Once the income qualifies under the former source it will not qualify again under the next source.

The sequence for Box 1 maintained by the law is:

– business income;
– income from employment and other independently performed services;
– investment income;
– periodic payments;
– taxable income from owner-occupied dwelling.

3.3 BOX 1: BUSINESS INCOME

3.3.1 General

Box 1 includes, as mentioned above, also profit from business activities.

The ITA does not contain a definition of a business but merely states that business income is received by the person for whose account an enterprise is carried on.

The question whether or not an enterprise exists may be important for determining the character of the income, as special rules apply for different sources (e.g., income from independently performed services rather than business profit). An enterprise is generally understood to be an organization of capital and labour which participates in the economic process for the purpose of making a profit. Examples are a trading company, a factory, a shop, a farm, etc. For the application of the ITA, a business also includes the independent professions (lawyers, accountants, etc.).

Not all assets owned by a taxpayer who carries on an enterprise are considered to be business assets. Depending on their function within the enterprise there can be distinguished assets which are compulsory business assets (machinery), or private assets (private home), whereas with regard to some assets the entrepreneur has a choice (private home partly used as shop, office, etc.). Once a certain choice has been made, the taxpayer cannot change such a choice unless the circumstances have changed. Only special circumstances may justify a change. A change which is not justified by qualifying special circumstances will be ignored for tax purposes so that the tax consequences will be based on the original choice. This may be important in the case of a sale; for example, a capital gain realized on the sale of a business asset will be taxable whereas the gain on the sale of a non-business asset will not be taxable. Specific rules have to be applied if the partner of an entrepreneur or some members of both their families provide assets to be used for the business. This is called business use scheme (*terbeschikkingsstellingsregeling*).

The Netherlands tax year is the calendar year, as mentioned above. Consequently, in most cases, the entrepreneur will calculate his or her profit for tax purposes on the basis of a financial year which is equal to a calendar year. It is, however, allowed (Article 3.66 ITA 2001) under certain conditions to adopt a financial year which deviates from the calendar year. The above only applies so long as the taxpayer regularly keeps books and closes the accounts on a regular yearly basis and provided the nature of the business justifies a financial year which differs from the calendar year. If such a financial year is accepted, the profit calculated on the sale thereof will be included in the tax year (calendar year) in which the financial year ends. A financial year exceeding 12 months will be split in two periods. The first will run 12 months provided that both periods end in different calendar years. The profit of the first year must be estimated and the balance will be allocated to the second year.

3.3.2 Definition of Profit

A distinction must be made between the total profit derived from an enterprise during its total existence (Article 3.8 ITA 2001) and the annual profit (Article 3.25 ITA 2001).

The definition of total profit is: the aggregate benefits derived from an enterprise under whatever name and in whatever form.

The definition of the annual profit is also very general. As to the annual profit, the law merely provides that the profit should be calculated in accordance with 'sound business practice' based on a consistent course. The calculation must be irrespective of the probable result and may only be modified if such a modification is justified according to 'sound business practice'.

It basically boils down to the difference between the equity in euro's at the beginning of the enterprise and the equity in euro's at the end, to be increased with withdrawals and to be decreased with equity contributions. In the Netherlands the fiscal balance sheet may be different from the commercial balance sheet. An example of withdrawals are withdrawals of money or goods for personal use.

3.3.3 Exemption from Profit

A number of exemptions are provided for in Articles 3.11–3.13 ITA 2001. Some of them apply to the calculation of taxable profit in general and consequently also apply to corporate taxpayers (see section 4.6.2). Others by their nature apply to individual taxpayers only.

The most important exemptions applying to individual income taxpayers are:

- the forestry exemption (Article 3.11 ITA 2001);
- agricultural exemptions (Article 3.12 ITA 2001);
- remissions of claims by creditors (Article 3.13 ITA 2001).

3.3.4 Exemption upon Termination of Business (Article 3.79 ITA 2001)

If an entrepreneur ceases his or her business activities, either through a liquidation or through a transfer of his or her business, the difference between the market value of the enterprise and the book value will be included in the taxable income to the extent that such profit exceeds the special exemption of EUR 3,630 (2011). The exemption does not apply to a partial termination of the business activities.

If a former termination has already absorbed a part of the exemption, only the rest can be used for another later termination.

3.3.5 Old Age Reserve

Private entrepreneurs, not older than 65, can reserve annually a certain amount to the old age reserve. The annual increase of the reserve is tax-exempt. The law provides for a minimum and maximum reservation based on a percentage of the profit.

The reserve may not exceed the net asset value in any tax year. The law provides for a number of occasions in which the reserve must be added to profit. In some cases the total reserve must be added to the taxable income (decease, emigration). The entrepreneur can at any time decide to convert his or her reserve into an annuity right.

3.3.6 Non-deductible or Partly Deductible Business Expenses

In the case of business profits, generally, all expenses incurred in the course of the business are deductible. However, some business expenses are not deductible, or only partly deductible. The threshold amount is EUR 4,300 (2011).

Not deductible expenses are:

- vessels used for representation purposes;
- office space in private homes, not belonging to the business assets, from, or in which, small part of the income is earned;
- clothing, with the exception of professional clothing;
- literature, with the exception of professional literature;
- word processors, computers and similar audio-visual equipment, not belonging to the business assets;
- fines and penalties imposed either by the Dutch judiciary (including tax fines and penalties) or by institutions of the EU.

Only 73.5% of the following expenses may be deducted:

- food, drink and stimulants, as well as cafeteria provisions, with some exceptions;
- congresses, symposia, seminars, educational trips and the like, including the related travel and lodging.

With respect to the costs of the use of a private car, which does not belong to the business assets, EUR 0,19 (2011) per kilometre is deductible.

The costs of housing outside one's own residence are deductible for a maximum of two years. Moving costs are deductible in an amount of up to EUR 7750 (2011) plus mover's fee.

3.3.7 Transfer and Liquidation of a Business

In the case of a liquidation an enterprise ceases to exist; in the case of a transfer another taxpayer will continue to carry on the business. At liquidation the various assets are sold separately but may also be partly or totally transferred from the taxpayer's business assets into his or her private assets. Partial termination of a business is deemed to take place if a substantial part of the enterprise is either liquidated or sold.

3.3.8 Termination of a Business

As mentioned in Article 3.8 ITA 2001 all benefits and losses derived from an enterprise will in principle be included in the business income. If, when and to what extent these profits and losses will be taken into account depends on the sound commercial practice concept (Article 3.25 ITA 2001). It is conceivable that certain profit elements will not be included in the business profit on an annual basis but inclusion is deferred. However, all these items will ultimately be taken into account at the event of termination; that is, at the time the taxpayer ceases to receive income from that enterprise because it will not be carried on for his or her account any more. It follows that the enterprise as such need not necessarily have ceased. It may, for example, have been sold to someone else who continues the business for his or her own account.

3.3.9 Calculation of the Termination Profit

The termination profit is calculated by a comparison of the balance sheet made in accordance with the normal rules as applied within the scope of sound commercial practice and by a special balance sheet in which all assets and liabilities are valued at market value. Article 3.63 ITA 2001 offers the opportunity to transfer an enterprise tax-free, provided a number of conditions are met. The enterprise has to be transferred to a partner or employee who has been a partner or an employee for the last 36 months before the moment of transfer. The successor has to replace his or her predecessor, which means he or she has, for example, to maintain the original book value, the same valuation of stocks and the same method of depreciation.

3.3.10 Termination through Divorce or Decease of the Taxpayer

Although upon death of the taxpayer there will be no transfer or sale of the enterprise, the enterprise will deemed to be terminated through a fictitious transfer to the heirs (Article 3.58, ITA 2001). The difference between market value (including goodwill) and book value will be included in the last return of the deceased taxpayer. Any successor will start with a new enterprise at market value. A similar fictitious transfer is deemed to occur where a taxpayer is married in community of goods and the marriage ends through divorce. The above-mentioned payment of tax through a fictitious transfer is not levied where a written request is made by the successors of the deceased or upon divorce. In that case the original book value has to be maintained (Article 3.6 ITA 2001).

3.3.11 Final Settlement

Article 3.60 ITA 2001 provides for a final settlement where a taxpayer carrying on a business in the Netherlands ceases to be taxable in the Netherlands. The law defines the profit resulting from this final settlement as any benefits from the business which have not yet been included in the annual profit or the profit derived from a transfer etc. (Article 3.61 ITA 2001, see the preceding paragraphs of this subchapter).

This final settlement will, for example, apply in the following circumstances:

(a) the taxpayer emigrates and continues his or her business in another country;
(b) a non-resident taxpayer transfers his or her business to another country;
(c) if a business is transferred.

3.3.12 Exemption in Case of a Transfer of a Business to a Company

The conversion of a private business or a partnership into a limited liability company (either a *Besloten Vennootschap* (BV) or *Naamloze Vennootschap* (NV)) will in principle constitute a taxable transfer. The taxation of profit resulting from such a transfer is not levied if the taxpayer so requests. The application, to be made under Article 3.65 ITA 2001, must be filed with the tax inspector. The request will be granted provided the taxpayer participates in the share capital of the company in the same or almost the same ratio as his or her share in the business, or partnership, and meets the conditions imposed by the Ministry. The conditions for a tax-exempt transfer under Article 3.65 ITA 2001 (generally referred to as the standard conditions) are published in the *Official Gazette* but may be adapted for each specific case. A detailed description of the various conditions is beyond the scope of this book. In general it can be said that the conditions are such as to assure the levy of income and corporate income tax as well as the collection thereof. Furthermore, special rules are included for the calculation of the issued and paid-up capital as well as concerning the non-transfer of the shares years after the transfer of the business to the company.

3.3.13 Partnerships

A partnership can be described as a legal form through which the various partners carry on a business under a common name. The most common from is the general partnership with each partner being separately liable for the partnership's debts. A less usual form is the limited partnership, where the general or managing partner is fully responsible for its debts but the limited partner is merely liable up to the amount of his or her capital contribution.

For tax purposes, a partnership is not treated as a separate legal entity but is considered transparent; that is, for tax purpose each of the partners is deemed to carry on a business for his or her share in the partnership. Consequently each partner may use his or her own system of profit calculation (within, of course, the scope of the sound business practice rules).

A limited partner will only be considered to carry on a business if the partnership itself carries on a business and he or she is entitled to the hidden reserves of the partnership.

3.3.14 Deductible Expenses

In the case of business profits generally, all expenses incurred in the course of the business are deductible, regardless of whether the expenses were necessary in the view of the tax authorities. In other words, the authorities may not interfere in business policy; they are not allowed to make a judgment as to whether the expenses were reasonable. As regards deductible expenses the rule is different. For instance, if an employee incurs certain costs, the reasonableness of those costs can be judged.

The wording of Article 3.108 ITA 2001 clearly indicates that the expenses must have been incurred in respect of the income derived from a certain source. Expenses incurred in respect of the acquisition of the source of income itself are not deductible. It is obvious that in many cases the distinction is not easy to make; for example, the legal costs of a lawsuit entered into by an employee to prevent his or her discharge from his or her employment were deemed to be incurred to maintain his or her income from the employment and were hence deductible – they were not incurred to maintain the source of the income: the employment.

3.4 BOX 1: OTHER INCOME FROM EMPLOYMENT AND DWELLING

3.4.1 General

For the determination of 'wage' and 'employment' reference is made to the relevant articles in the Wage Tax Act (see Chapter 5). For the application of the income tax, wages will in principle be subject to income tax as employment income. Wage tax is withheld from wages, salaries and other benefits, in cash or in kind, arising from present or former employment. Also some periodic payments such as, for example, state old age pension (*Algemene Ouderdomswet* (AOW)) are subject to wages tax. Certain expense allowances necessary to meet the expenses incurred in the course of the employment are not included in the wage tax computation (except of course to the extent they are considered excessive). Income from employment may, however, also include income which is not subject to wages tax such as tips or on request income from an employment with a non-resident employer who does not maintain a permanent establishment in the Netherlands and consequently is not required to withhold wages tax.

When an employer puts a car at the employee's disposal and the costs connected with the car are borne by the employer, the employee must add between 5% and 35% of the Netherlands catalogue value of the car to his or her taxable yearly income. The percentage varies and is depending of the degree of air pollution the car provokes.

3.4.2 Some Categories of Non-deductible or Partly Deductible Expenses for Non-business Income

A lot of expenses are not deductible, or only partly deductible. These expenses are mentioned in the Wage Tax Act. The income tax follows the same rules as the wage tax.

3.4.3 Moment of Taxation

Special rules apply to determine when this kind of income was actually received. These rules are based on the principle that the income has not been received unless the taxpayer can in fact dispose of the income. This is deemed to be the case if:

(a) the income has been actually received, or has been credited; has been put at the disposal of the taxpayer; has become interest-bearing; or
(b) the income can be claimed and collected without further difficulties.

If income is received on a conditional basis, a distinction must be made between a condition subsequent and a condition precedent. In the first case the contract is completed but dissolved at a later stage because of the fulfilment of a condition. Income received under such a condition is deemed to be received immediately. Any repayment will be considered negative income. In the case of a condition precedent a contract is only completed once the condition is satisfied. Income subject to a condition precedent is deemed to be received only after this condition has been satisfied.

Income in kind is taken into account at market value. This will generally be the sales value. In those cases where the income cannot be exchanged for cash or where it is unusual to do so the value will at most be based on the amount saved by the taxpayer. For some categories such as free living, heating, light, water, etc., fixed amounts have been established.

3.4.4 Income from Independently Performed Services

Only income from activities and services which do not qualify as income from employment or profit derived from an enterprise can be considered as income from independently performed services. In order to qualify as such, a number of conditions must be met. Although they do not need to have been considerable, a certain degree of activity is required. This activity does not necessarily need to be carried out by the taxpayer himself or herself but can be carried out by a third party on his or her behalf. There must be a reasonable expectation that the activities will produce income. Examples of this income category are income from operating a lodging house, fees for services, income received from copyrights, or patents, or income from the disposal of such rights by the authors or investors themselves.

This does not apply to their legal successors; for example, their heirs. For them the patent or copyright becomes a private asset which will be taxed according to the rules of Box 3. The disposal of the rights by the heirs is tax-exempt.

3.4.5 OWNER-OCCUPIED DWELLINGS

Special rules apply for the calculation of an imputed rental value for property occupied by the owner.

3.4.5.1 Rental Value

The imputed rental value is based on the real estate tax value of the property and taxed in Box 1. For most houses the rental value will be 0,55% of the real estate tax value (if that value is between EUR 75,000 and EUR 1,020,000). The minimum rental value is nil (if the value is less than EUR 12,500); the maximum rental value for houses over EUR 1,010,000 is EUR 5,555 plus 1.05% of the value over EUR 1,010,000. No expenses other than mortgage interest and the costs of mortgage and leasehold charges, if any, can be deducted.

The income from the rent of rooms is exempt if the rent does not exceed EUR 4,333 (2011) per annum, provided a number of requirements are met. For example, the room that is rented has to be part of the house in which the owner lives and may not be a complete entity itself. If the income out of renting exceeds the amount mentioned this income will be taxed in Box 3.

3.4.6 DEDUCTION OF PREMIUMS FOR PERIODIC PAYMENTS

The most important type of special expenses is the life annuity premium. Under certain conditions these premiums for life insurances and pensions can be deducted in Box 1, depending on the income and pension already accrued (in some cases the payments will be taxed later on). Payments to non-resident insurance companies are only deductible under special circumstances; for example, if the taxpayer previously immigrated to the Netherlands. If the premium is deductible, the later payments out of this life insurance will be taxed as periodic payments in Box 1.

3.4.7 INCOME FROM PERIODIC PAYMENTS

Apart from the periodic payments mentioned above (for which there was premium deduction), some other periodic payments are also taxed.

The law recognizes four categories of periodic payments in this respect, that is:

(a) periodic payments provided for under public law; for instance, public scholarship payments;
(b) periodic payments based on family law except payments derived from relatives in the first and second degree, for example alimony payments from the ex-partner;

(c) any other periodic payments which can be legally claimed as not being periodic payments qualifying as investment income, unless the recipient has a certain family relation with the payer;
(d) periodic payments made by legal entities so far as they cannot be legally claimed.

Certain government subsidies and a part of the government paid public scholarship payment (*Studiefinanciering*), which would qualify as a periodic payment, are, under certain conditions, tax exempt.

Deductible expenses are those expenses which are deductible from the income derived from the various sources in order to arrive at the net income from those sources. They do not apply to business profits or to capital gains from a substantial interest.

3.4.8 Mortgage-Linked Endowment Insurance

Recently the so-called mortgage-linked endowment insurance has gained more importance. This insurance consists of a life insurance related to a mortgage. This is an interesting instrument for taxpayers because the interest paid on the mortgage on the owner-occupied dwellings is deductible in Box 1. While the interest gained on the insurance capital over the years, if certain conditions are met, is tax-exempt. At the end of the period agreed upon (mostly 30 years), or the moment of decease of the insured or his or her partner in between, the insured capital has to be used to repay the mortgage.

There are some conditions, one of them is that there has to be a contract and in it, it has to be stipulated that the money out of the insurance will only be used to repay the mortgage or other debts made to acquire the dwellings. If all conditions are met, the money paid out of the insurance, including the interest, will not be taxed (but the interest paid on the mortgage is tax deductible). All other insurance policies will be taxed in Box 3.

3.4.9 Negative Personal Allowance

3.4.9.1 General

Negative personal allowances are deductible from the total income in Box 1. These allowances do not have a relationship with the acquisition of income. Payments qualifying as such are deductible by the payer and are sometimes taxable in the hands of the payee. For deduction certain conditions must be met. There are also maxima. There are also several threshold amounts mentioned in the law.

3.4.9.2 Categories of Negative Personal Allowances

(1) Payments for expenses for maintenance for a small group of family members, as well as their lump sum payments.

(2) Payments to children under the age of 27 can be deductible, if the taxpayer does not receive child allowances under the General Child Allowance Act and the child itself does not receive government's public scholarship payment (*Studiefinanciering*). The deductable amounts are fixed and depend on the age of the child and the total costs paid for supporting the child.
(3) Medical expenses. The most important category in practice is payments in connection with sickness and disablement. However, the expenses are only deductible to a certain extent.
(4) Expenditures for handicapped children who normally live in an institution, but who are visiting their families in the weekends.
(5) Training or study costs. Only the costs incurred in connection with training or studies for the profession of the taxpayer or his or her partner are deductible. Study as a hobby does not qualify. Studies which are made to maintain the level of knowledge necessary to carry out a certain profession do not qualify as extraordinary expenses. Only study expenses for a new job or profession qualify. To these costs certain limits apply.
(6) Payments for listed historical buildings.
(7) Gifts made to qualifying social welfare institutions are deductible. Gifts to non-resident institutions are sometimes also deductible, provided a number of requirements are met. Gifts are only deductible in the income tax if the total amount of the gifts exceeds 1% of the total taxable income (with a minimum of EUR 60). Deductible gifts cannot exceed 10% of the total taxable income. This limitation does not apply to gifts by means of life annuity payments to the institutions referred to above, as well as to certain other associations, provided certain conditions are met. As to the moment of deduction, the same rules apply as for deductible expenses and extraordinary expenses.

The expenses will be taken into account at the time they are either paid directly, through set-off, or if the taxpayer has put them at someone's disposal, or if they become interest bearing.

3.4.9.3 Moment of Deduction

Payments qualify for deduction at the time they are either paid directly, through set-off, or at the time the taxpayer has put them at someone's disposal or they have become interest-bearing.

3.5 BOX 2: GAINS FROM A SUBSTANTIAL INTEREST IN A COMPANY

Individuals are not subject to tax on capital gains unless the gain is realized within an enterprise, qualifies as income from independently performed services, or is derived from the sale of a substantial interest (see below).

3.5.1 Introduction/Definition

The shareholder, natural person, who, together with his or her partner or on his or her own, either directly or indirectly, owns 5% or more of the shares in a company, has a substantial interest (*aanmerkelijk belang*). Dividends and benefits derived from disposal will be taxed at a fixed rate of 25%. Some family members who own less than 5% can also have a substantial interest in a company, if a relative in the ascending or descending line owns a substantial interest in this company.

If the company has different kind of shares, and the shareholder has a substantial interest in one kind of these shares, then his or her shares of a kind in which no substantial interest is being hold, will also become part of the substantial interest.

Not only shares, but also options to buy 5% or more of the shares in a company can form a substantial interest as well.

The income from substantial interest can be regular income or income from alienation. Both kinds of incomes are taxed in Box 2.

The difference between these two lies in the moment of taxation. Regular income is taxed at the moment the shareholder receives this income, while income out of alienation is taxed at the moment of disposal, in most cases this is the moment when the sales contract of the shares is concluded.

If a shareholder has a substantial interest in a company, profit-sharing certificates or other types of shares issued by that same company are deemed to be part of the substantial interest, this is called the *meesleepregeling*. Non-residents will only have to pay tax in Box 2 if they have substantial interest in a company established in the Netherlands.

3.5.2 Regular Income

Regular income is income less costs.

Regular income consists not only of dividend, but also of other kinds of distributions, such as disguised profit distributions, stock dividends (shares) and repayments of capital. Disguised profit distributions are those distributions which try to conceal a distribution; for example, a sale of assets to the shareholder for an amount less than the market value. Income in the form of stock dividends is valued at zero, and that will also be the value of the acquisition price. The average value of the total shares will then go down. A repayment of capital is income, unless the paid-up issued capital has been reduced accordingly by an official change of the deed of incorporation and is less than the acquisition price. The acquisition price will be diminished with a tax-free repayment of capital. Regular income is taxed at the moment the shareholder receives his or her income or at the moment his or her income will yield interest.

3.5.3 The Income of Alienation

If the shareholder alienates his or her shares wholly or partially he or she also generates income in Box 2. Income from alienation is the difference between the transfer price and the acquisition price. The acquisition price of one share is the average value of all shares. Alienation covers sales and a variety of other activities in which the shares are transferred. For example, purchases of shares by the company itself, amounts received in connection with the liquidation of a company, mergers, divisions, inheritance, marriage, divorce and emigration.

Shares that form no longer a substantial interest are fictitiously alienated.

Where there is no consideration or, for example, the sale has not been effected under arm's length conditions, the actual market price will be taken into account.

There are two exceptions to the rule that income of alienation is taxed at the moment of alienation. In case the payment is based on an earning scheme, the transfer price is based on the estimated receipts. Less or more receipts lead to an adjustment of the income of alienation. A readjustment of the transfer price, based on an agreement, can also adjust the income of alienation. A higher price means positive income of alienation, while a lower one forms negative income.

The law offers special provisions for some specific ways of alienation, in which case no income is subject to taxation. These schemes imply that the acquisition price of the former owner becomes the acquisition price of the new owner, so that the tax claim moves from one owner to the next one (e.g., if the shares are inherited, see section 3.5.5).

3.5.4 Reorganization Schemes

In case of qualifying mergers (stock merger and legal merger) and divisions, specific rules provide for exemption of tax. These rules partly are an incorporation of the EU Merger Directive.

Mergers, in which companies from the Netherlands or two EU Member States are involved, will be entitled to these provisions, if they fulfil a number of terms and conditions. The acquiring company has to obtain a majority of the voting rights in the other company in exchange of their shares. Within the framework of the exchange of shares, an amount in cash not exceeding 10% of the nominal value of the shares issued in exchange may be paid. This additional cash payment will be taxed.

Divisions are also entitled to the provision mentioned above, including the cash payment.

Both mergers and division will not be entitled to the facility if the merger or division has as its principal objective (or as one of its principal objectives) tax evasion or tax avoidance. Also if it is not carried out for valid commercial reasons such as restructuring or rationalization of the activities of the companies participating in the operation may constitute a presumption that the operation has tax evasion or tax avoidance as its principal objective (or one as of its principal objectives).

3.5.5 Marriage, Divorce, Inheritance and Donation

A number of transfers, often within the family, take place without payment. Paying taxation without receiving payment for the transfer can cause enormous liquidity problems. The law offers specific provisions for alienations originating from marriage, divorce, inheritance and donation.

Marriage and divorce only leads to income of alienation if the substantial interest is held in joint ownership, as under a general community property regime. The alienations caused by marriage or divorce will in general all be tax-free, provided the acquisition prices of the (received) shares remain those of the former owner. Voluntary payment is possible at request.

The inheritance of shares in a company which owns business assets and investment assets, is only free for the part of the alienation corresponding with the value of the business assets, together with 5% of the value of investments assets, if present. The division of the inheritance is tax-free, but if it takes a period longer than two years, the over distribution is a taxable alienation.

The donation of a substantial interest is an alienation. Donations of a substantial interest in a company, in which the beneficiary has been working for a period of two years or more, can be tax-free, if a number of terms and conditions are met, in which case the acquisition price of the beneficiary will be that of the donator. If the company owns not only business assets but investment assets as well, the alienation is partial tax-free just as in case of inheritance (see above).

3.5.6 Emigration

Emigration of the substantial interest holder is considered to be an alienation. However, deferment of payment of taxation is possible under specific terms and conditions. An alienation taking place within a period ten years after emigration leads to payment, unless an agreement on the avoidance of double taxation prohibits such taxation. Ten years after the emigration the deferment expires and the substantial interests can be sold without payment of taxes in Box 2.

3.5.7 Shares Losing Their Substantial Interest Qualification

Shares can lose their substantial interest qualification due to an emission, a merger or a (partial) sale. The (remaining) shares are alienated fictitiously, but if the shareholder opts for non-alienation, the shares will remain a so-called fictitious substantial interest, to be taxed at the moment of alienation or at the moment the shareholders decide the shares form no longer a fictitious substantial interest.

3.5.8 Liquidation of a Company

The liquidation of a company is a fictitious alienation. Amounts received in connection with the liquidation of a company less the acquisition price are income of alienation. Consequently, the acquisition price is diminished with the amount that was no income of alienation.

3.5.9 Losses

A negative income is a loss out of substantial interest. This loss can be carried back one year or carried forward during a nine years period. In principal, this loss can only be compensated with income out of a substantial interest. If, however, no substantial interest exists during a two years period, this loss can be turned into a tax credit to be compensated with taxation on other income, in other boxes, than income out of substantial interest.

3.6 BOX 3: INCOME FROM SAVINGS AND INVESTMENTS

3.6.1 General

Examples of assets taxed in Box 3 are:

(1) savings;
(2) second homes and let property;
(3) shares, not forming a substantial interest.

Minus debts that are not taxed in Box 1 or 2.

Examples of assets that *do not* fall in Box 3 are:

(1) owners occupied dwellings;
(2) passenger cars, furniture and other things for personal use;
(3) ethical investments to a certain amount.

The net assets in Box 3 are deemed to generate an income of 4%, which is taxed at a fixed percentage of 30%. As a consequence the really received interest (or other income out of these assets) is exempt. So the real income derived from tangible property is not taxable as well, only the value of the property itself is taken into account.

The assets and debts are valued at market value. These values are noted on the first of January of that year. There is a personal tax-exempt. This exempt depends on the age of the person and also of the fact if he or she has children under the age of 18 in his or her custody. The exempt standard amount is EUR 20,785 (2011).

3.6.2 Benefit in Kind

Benefits received in kind will be included in taxable income on the basis of the market value of the benefits. If it concerns items which cannot be (or as a rule are not) sold, the income will be deemed not to be higher than the amount the recipient is deemed to save through this payment in kind. For the valuation special rules apply (see also Chapter 5, Wage Tax).

3.6.3 Allocation and Moment of Deduction

Deductible expenses must be allocated to the various types of income to which they apply.

Prepaid expenses. Generally, expenses must be deducted in the year in which they are incurred. This does not necessarily mean that they are only taken into account once paid. The expenses will be taken into account at the time they are either paid directly, through set-off, or if the taxpayer has put them at someone's disposal, or if they have become interest-bearing.

A special provision is made for the deduction of interest paid in advance, sometimes they are allocated to the year concerning.

3.7 LOSS RELIEF

3.7.1 General

Chapter IV (Articles 3.150 and 4.49 ITA 2001) provides for the compensation of losses; that is, the compensation of a loss or negative income incurred in a given year with positive income of another year ('vertical compensation' of losses). Negative income from different sources within a certain year is first compensated with the positive income in the same box and in the same year ('horizontal compensation'). Losses can be carried forward as well as carried back.

3.7.1.1 Initial Losses

Initial losses are incurred by a business during the first six years of the existence of the business. Provided that the taxpayer regularly keeps his or her books with annual balance sheets, the initial losses can be carried forward indefinitely. The amount of the initial losses is to be established by a formal decision of the inspector.

3.7.1.2 Carry-Forward/Carry-Back: Order of Set-Off

Losses in Box 1 can be carried back three years and carried forward nine years. For losses in Box 2 it is one year back and nine years forward. In Box 3 there cannot be losses.

3.8 MISCELLANEOUS

3.8.1 Averaging Income

Domestic taxpayers under the age of 65 may, under certain conditions, request that their income earned over a period of three years will be re-allocated equally to those years. The difference between the tax actually paid and the tax due on the basis of this reallocation is refunded, provided the difference exceeds EUR 545 (2011).

3.8.2 Assessment Limitations

Income tax is levied through an assessment. If an individual receives income qualifying under any of the boxes described in the various paragraphs above, an assessment will be made out, whereas prepaid taxes, such as wages tax and (dividend) withholding tax, will be credited or, as the case may be, refunded. There are, however, some exceptions to this rule:

(1) according to Article 9.4 ITA 2001, no assessment will be made if no tax is due; or
(2) if the additional taxes to be paid do not exceed EUR 44.

In these cases the prepaid wage tax and withholding tax are final.

Amounts less than EUR 14 will not be refunded. If the amount is higher, a taxpayer is entitled to a refund.

3.8.3 Tax Credit

For income derived from employment a standard deduction for general expenses is allowed. The employed person's maximum tax credit (*arbeidskorting*) for 2011 is, depending of the age of the person, EUR 2,362. The general tax credit (*algemene heffingskorting*) for every taxpayer is for 2011 EUR 1,987.

Chapter 4
Corporate Income Tax

4.1 GENERAL

The present corporate income tax is levied on the basis of the CITA 69. For many years Netherlands corporate income tax was part of the so-called classical system, which means that income is taxed both at company level (corporate income tax) as well as at shareholder level after distribution (withholding tax, income tax).

Subject to corporate income tax are domestic and non-resident taxpayers. Domestic taxpayers are companies (usually corporate bodies) that are resident in the Netherlands (Article 2 CITA 69). They are subject to tax on their worldwide income (although relief for foreign-source income may be given). Non-resident taxpayers are companies that are not residents of the Netherlands (Article 3 CITA 69). They are subject to the Netherlands corporate income tax only if and to the extent that they derive income from Netherlands sources as defined in Article 17 CITA 69 (see section 4.12).

The answer to the question whether or not a company is resident of the Netherlands is given, although in general terms, in Article 4 GTA. According to Article 4 GTA the place of residence of a company is determined by circumstances. The factual circumstances are decisive. The most important factor is the place of effective management, but other factors such as the head office location, the place where the meetings of shareholders are held and the place where company records are kept, etc., may also be of importance.

The CITA 69 itself does not contain a definition of residence. If however a company is incorporated under Netherlands law it is deemed to be a resident taxpayer in the Netherlands (Article 2 paragraph 4, CITA 69). Article 2 paragraph 4, CITA 69 may cause a Netherlands company to be resident of the Netherlands although its place of effective management is in another state (dual resident company). This effect of Article 2 paragraph 4, CITA 69 can be limited under the terms of a tax treaty. In that case, a tie-breaker rule may divide the tax base of the company between the state where the place of effective management of the taxpayer is located and the state of incorporation. In that case the respective other state may not include in its tax base the income which is attributed to the first state.

4.2 TAXABLE ENTITIES

The corporate income tax only applies to certain companies (*lichamen*). The law does not give a definition of company in this respect. According to the enumeration in Articles 2 (domestic taxpayers) and 3 (non-resident taxpayers) CITA 69, not all companies are legal entities.

4.2.1 The Domestic Taxpayers

According to Article 2 CITA 69, the following companies that are resident of the Netherlands are subject to the tax:

(a) public limited companies (NV's) as well as private limited companies (BV's), other stock companies and open limited partnerships (*open commanditaire vennootschappen*);
(b) cooperatives including cooperative societies;
(c) mutual insurance companies and associations which act as mutual insurance companies or mutual credit institutions;
(d) societies and foundations which qualify as institutions concerned with public housing;
(e) certain other associations and other than public corporations not referred to under (a), (b), (c) and (d) if and to the extent that they carry on a business;
(f) investment funds *(fondsen voor gemene rekening);*
(g) certain specifically mentioned government entities such as agricultural enterprises and industrial and transport enterprises with the exception of water companies and municipal transport companies.

The underlying idea is that any company which carries on a business (with the exception of individuals and associations of individuals, such as partnerships) should be subject to corporate income tax. The entities referred to under (a), (b), (c) and (d) are deemed to carry on a business. The entities under (e) are merely subject to tax if and to the extent that a business is carried on. This will automatically be assumed if the purpose of the entity is to make a profit. From Article 4 CITA 69 follows further that an entity is assumed to carry on a business when it competes with a business carried on by an individual or the companies referred to under (a), (b), (c) and (d). Competition is defined by the courts as those activities which affect sales or turnover of existing businesses and does not necessarily include the intention to compete.

Under certain conditions, pension funds, companies providing for medical care and public libraries are exempt from corporate income tax (Articles 5 and 6 CITA 69).

4.2.2 Foreign Taxpayers

Article 3 CITA 69 provides that certain non-resident entities are also subject to Netherlands corporate income tax provided these entities receive domestic income as defined in Article 17 CITA 69.

The foreign entities are:

(a) associations and other legal entities;
(b) open limited partnerships and other partnerships with a capital divided into shares but without legal personality; and
(c) *doelvermogens*, this is a term which is not further defined but which covers a wide variety of entities. Examples are certain funds, trusts and foundations.

4.3 DEFINITION OF BUSINESS INCOME (DOMESTIC TAXPAYERS)

4.3.1 General

The CITA 1969 does not provide for a special definition of business income but merely refers to the relevant Articles of the ITA 2001. There are basically two types of exceptions to this:

- those specifically provided for in the CITA 1969; and
- those differences which automatically follow from the difference in nature between an individual and a company subject to corporate income tax.

4.3.1.1 The Tax Base

The tax base is the so-called 'taxable amount' (*belastbaar bedrag*). The taxable amount is defined as the annual 'taxable profit' less the loss relief available under Chapter IV of the CITA 1969. Taxable profit is profit less deductible gifts, or, schematically:

Profit a
  exempt profit and charitable contributions __*b*__
Taxable profit a–b
  less: tax losses _ *c*__
taxable amount *a-b-c*

4.3.1.2 The Tax Year

The tax year for resident taxpayers is the accounting year, which can differ from the calendar year, provided regular book-keeping is maintained. As of 2011, the same applies to non-resident taxpayers.

4.3.1.3 Calculation of Business Income

Business income includes all types of income from business in the Netherlands or elsewhere. No distinction is made between capital gains and ordinary profits. Article 3.8 ITA 2001 provides for the general concept of business income, that is the total business income whereas Article 3.25 ITA 2001 sets forth the annual business income concept, that is the allocation of total business income to the appropriate tax years. Business income must be calculated in euros.

The tax accounts, which are based on the commercial accounts with certain adjustments, will be filed together with the annual tax return. The return itself provides for a special method of calculation based on the annual increase or decrease in the equity, which can be summarized as follows:

equity at the end of the tax year			□ □ □
less:	equity at the beginning of the tax year		□ □ □–
equity increase (or decrease)			■ ■ ■
plus:	withdrawals (e.g., repayments of capital, corporate income tax, dividends)	□ □ □	
less:	equity contributions	□ □ □	
less:	exempt profit items	□ □ □	
plus/less:	alterations in the fiscal reserves	□ □ □	
profit			□ □ □±
			■ ■ ■

It goes without saying that the profit calculated by this method should be the same as the profit shown in the accounts. In this respect it is noted that tax accounting is as a rule based on the accrual method. There may be some exceptions in the case of small businesses.

4.3.1.4 Capital Contributions and Withdrawals or Distributions

Capital contributions are excluded from profit and – correspondingly – repayments of capital and distributions of profits are not deductible.

Not only payments on shares issued (par value and surplus) are recognized as capital but also so-called ‘informal capital contributions’.

If a parent company grants a benefit to a subsidiary, without shares being issued and without any business reason, which under similar circumstances would not have been granted to independent third parties, such benefit is excluded from the subsidiary’s profit as being an ‘informal capital contribution’.

The opposite of the above-mentioned contribution to capital is the withdrawal or distribution. Generally speaking, it can be said that a withdrawal or distribution is any payment which is not made within the scope of the business activity but is a disposition of equity or profit among or on behalf of the shareholders. Examples – but this is not an exhaustive list – are mentioned in Article 10 CITA 69. Article 10 CITA 69 mentions, for example, dividend distributions in general, directly or indirectly; the corporate income tax itself; the Netherlands dividend withholding tax (if not deducted from a dividend) and the lottery tax. In practice distributions of profits can be excessive salaries or pension rights to directors/shareholders; interest-free loans to a shareholder; transactions with related parties which are not at arm's length, etc. A special provision is made in Article 11 CITA 69. This article limits the deduction of fees paid to members of the supervisory board of a company who also hold a so-called substantial interest in the company. To the extent that the remuneration exceeds EUR 1,815 (2011), 50% (with a minimum of EUR 1,815) is deductible. The deductible amount cannot exceed EUR 9,076 (2011) per year. The non-deductible part will be considered a deemed dividend distribution.

4.3.2 Annual Business Income and Sound Business Practice

4.3.2.1 General

Article 3.25 ITA 2001 provides for the general principle that annual business income should be calculated in accordance with 'sound business practice', based on consistent principles. The calculation must be applied irrespective of the probable result and may only be changed if such a change is consistent with 'sound business practice' (see section 4.3.2.5, for a more detailed analysis of the concept of 'sound business practice'.

The term 'sound business practice' is not further defined by statute. This has resulted in a great amount of case law. Based on this case law, as a general rule, accounting methods based on generally accepted business economic principles are deemed to fall within the scope of the sound business practice concept. However, this will not be the case if they violate any provisions of the tax law or are not in accordance with the general principles on which the tax law is based. For instance, depreciation on the basis of replacement value is not allowed.

4.3.2.2 Prudence

An important element of the fiscal sound business practice concept is the element of prudence. From this principle follows, that losses may be deducted when expected but before realized, whereas profits do not have to be brought into account until actually realized.

4.3.2.3 Consistency

Another important element of the annual business income calculation is the rule of consistency. An adopted system may only be modified if such a modification is justified by 'sound business practice'. In principle, it can be said that the replacement of one method of accounting by another method is acceptable as long as both methods are in accordance with the 'sound business practice' concept, except where an incidental tax advantage is the objective, for example because of a change in tax rules through which certain profits would be taxed at a lower rate. However, the mere fact that the change in accounting method results in a loss does not in itself prevents such a change.

4.3.2.4 Continuity

The last requirement is that the accounting method adopted by the taxpayer should be followed without regard to the probable result. It could be said that this requirement in fact follows from others which have already been discussed (e.g., the consistency rule would already prevent an annual change purely based on retrieving incidental tax advantages). The principle of continuity of balance sheets is of particular importance where in a certain year a mistake or error from previous years is discovered; that is, if certain assets or liabilities have erroneously not been booked. According to the case law of the Supreme Court, such an error should give rise to an adjustment of business income in the years in which the error was made. If it is not possible to levy an additional assessment over some of the relevant years – the competence to levy an assessment for those years may have expired – the adjustment for those years will be made in the return of the latest year for which no assessment has been issued yet.

4.3.2.5 Sound Business Practice and Generally Accepted Accounting Principles

From the above it is evident that the concept of sound business practice is not necessarily identical with generally accepted accounting principles.

In determining the taxable profit, the statutory accounts should always be tested against the concept of sound business practice as interpreted by the Supreme Court. On the other hand, the taxpayer is not bound by the statutory accounts in calculating his or her taxable profit. If he or she applies a valuation system in the statutory accounts which would be acceptable for taxation purposes, he or she may use a more conservative system in the tax return provided that system is also acceptable. Accordingly, the creation of allowable provisions is not dependent on the statutory accounts.

4.3.3 Valuation of Assets

As a general rule, assets and liabilities must be valued as of the balance sheet date. Events occurring after the balance sheet date are not taken into consideration, with the exception of those events which arise from circumstances already in existence on the balance sheet date.

4.3.3.1 Receivables

Within the concept of sound business practice, receivables must be booked not later than the moment of completion of the transaction (delivery of goods, supply of services) from which they arise. It is permissible to book a receivable as soon as the sales contract is entered into. For valuation purposes it is permissible to take into account various items such as the terms of the receivable, whether interest will be received, the interest rate, etc.

Generally one can say that short-term receivables or receivables which can be claimed immediately or upon short notice will be valued at face value. Non-interest-bearing long-term receivables may be discounted.

Receivables in foreign currency must be valued in euros. In the case of long-term receivables in foreign currency, it is not necessary to account for a profit if the value of the foreign currency on the balance sheet date has increased against the euro, unless there is a material change in the currency exchange rate which is of a more permanent nature.

With respect to the valuation of receivables from insolvent debtors, two systems are possible:

- individual valuation; that is, any receivable will be individually valued, all specific circumstances in relation with this debtor will be taken into account;
- general valuation; that is, based on experience, a certain percentage may be deducted from the total of the receivables.

The decrease in value on the basis of these two systems can either be effected by decreasing the total amount of the receivables directly or by creating a special provision for bad debts.

According to the Supreme Court, the second system is only acceptable where there is a large number of debtors. If these are small in number and an individual valuation is possible, the system of individual valuation must be followed. On the basis of the case law it is also conceivable that a combination of both systems might be used; that is, a number of insolvent debtors are valued individually whereas the balance is valued by the deduction of a general percentage.

However, this percentage cannot be applied to receivables which have already been individually valued.

4.3.3.2 Cash

Cash must be valued at nominal value. Foreign currency must be valued at the official exchange rate on the balance sheet date.

An exception may occur where foreign exchange control laws prevent the exchange into euro. In such a case these circumstances, which could result in an exchange rate lower than the official exchange rate, may be taken into account.

4.3.3.3 Inventory

The inventory includes not only goods for sale but also raw materials, semi-manufactured articles and goods which are to be processed. In general it includes all goods within the company which contribute to its turnover.

According to the Supreme Court not all systems of valuing inventory on the basis of generally accepted accounting principles are acceptable from a tax point of view. This applies in particular to the system based on replacement value:

(a) *Cost*: The system of valuation at cost can be in accordance with sound business practice, unless the cost price is substantially above the real market value. Therefore, in practice, generally system (b) below will be chosen. In this respect the question arises which costs should be included in the cost price. In 1956 the Supreme Court held that the value of inventories of ready-made articles or semi-manufactured articles on the balance sheet should not include the fixed general overhead expenses. The basic consideration was that the cost price of those articles manufactured in the business itself should only include the costs which were directly connected with production. In later decisions this direct cost concept has been developed further. For instance, depreciation costs of machinery directly used to produce the articles is included in the cost price. The same applies to the wages of the employees working in the production department. It follows that other expenses can be directly charged to the profit and loss account. Examples of these are salaries, director's fees, housing expenses, storage costs.

(b) *The lower of cost or market value*: This is the most commonly applied system. The basis for this system is of course the cost price as discussed under (a) above. If, however, due to fluctuations in the market, the market price is lower, then the lower market value may be taken. Subsequent increases in market value will lead to a higher valuation until the historic cost price has again been reached.

(c) *Fifo/Lifo and base stock system*: In determining the cost of the inventory a first in/first out system or a last in/first out system may be applied.

Another system which under certain conditions is accepted by the courts is the so-called 'base stock system'. This system is founded on the theory that a company should have a normal or base stock, being the stock necessary to continue an undisturbed manufacturing process. This stock will be capitalized on the balance sheet at a fixed base price, to be defined as the price paid for the inventory at the beginning of the year in which the base stock system was established. Consequently, price increases in this base stock will have no effect on the book value of this stock. If at the balance sheet date the actual inventory is smaller than the base stock, a shortfall stock reserve, the amount necessary to replenish the actual inventory up to the level of the stock base, can be formed (*manco reserve*). This reserve will be the difference between the actual market price and the fixed base price of the goods. This reserve may be deducted from the book value of the base stock. If there is a surplus stock it can be valued at the lower of cost or market value.

The base stock system cannot be applied to all types of goods. According to the Supreme Court the base stock must consist of the same or similar goods as the ones existing at the time the base stock system was adopted by the company.

Finally it should be noted that the base stock system is applied not only to the stock actually held by the company, but also to the quantities of goods ordered. However, stock increase due to seasonal operations may not be taken into account. Despite the fact that the 'base stock system' is not allowed by International Financial Reporting Standards (IFRS) for the commercial accounts, in 2005 the Supreme Court stated that it can be allowed for calculating the taxable amount.

4.3.3.4 Work in Progress

Work in progress as discussed in this paragraph does not include semi-manufactured goods in a factory; to those the systems discussed under section 4.3.3.3 apply. Work in progress is generally merely of importance for the professions of, for example, lawyers, accountants and architects.

Work in progress includes undertaking of work (*aanneming van werk*) and contracting assignments (*onderhanden opdrachten*). As of 2007 work in progress has to be valued at the part corresponding with the fee that can be attributed to the completed part of the work in progress.

4.3.3.5 Fixed Assets

In several cases the Supreme Court has established that fixed assets are those assets which are to be used to carry on a trade or a business, as opposed to those assets which are intended for turnover. Fixed assets do not include articles which are to be used for maintenance, assets which are consumed in a short period, or those assets which have a low value.

In order to qualify as a business asset it is not necessary that the asset is legally owned, since 'economic ownership' qualifies in this respect, too. The concept of economic ownership has been developed in the tax case law because the legal owner is not always the one who has an economic interest in the property, which bears the risk of declination in value, damage or loss. An example is the buyer under a hire-purchase agreement who is not the juridical owner but who bears all risks. Consequently, the asset purchased under such an agreement is capitalized and depreciated in the books of the hire-purchaser. In the past the concept of 'economic ownership' often applied to joint business ventures where one of the partners, who remained the legal owner, contributed the use of the asset to the joint venture. In this respect it is pointed out that an asset also exists if, for example, a lessee makes considerable investments in or improvements to a leased property. Under Netherlands law, however, the owner of the property automatically becomes the owner of the investments or improvements, and hence bears the risk of changes in value. Therefore, the lessee is not the 'economic owner'. The Supreme Court has held, however, that the investment in the lease also qualifies as a separate asset and consequently must be depreciated by the lessee.

4.3.3.5.1 *Manufacturing and Acquisition Cost, Capitalized Expenditure*

In principle the acquisition costs of an asset includes all costs incurred in order to acquire the asset, as well as those, if any, necessary to make it ready for use. Acquisition costs does not include government subsidies or investment premiums. If the asset is produced by the company itself, the acquisition costs are the cost of production. In such a case, contrary to the position with regard to the inventory (see section 4.3.3.3), the total cost price – including the fixed general overhead expenses – must be taken into account. The question whether expenses must be capitalized or not can of course be rather important since in case of capitalization the expenses cannot be deducted totally in one year but are, through depreciation, allocated to a number of subsequent years. Important examples of capitalized expenditure are research costs which have resulted in a license, and advertising costs if they apply to an advertising campaign of more than a year.

4.3.3.5.2 *Depreciation*

Article 3.30 ITA 2001 provides for compulsory depreciation for tax purposes. It generally provides that annual depreciation amounts to that part of the acquisition or manufacturing cost not previously depreciated which can be attributed to the year. Depreciation does not start at the moment of acquisition but only starts when the business asset is put into use. Under the sound business practice concept various depreciation methods may be followed provided, however, that the method is in accordance with sound business practice and is consistently applied.

Changes in methods of depreciation are also allowed only if they are in accordance with sound business practice.

In order to calculate annual depreciation, the following items must be taken into account: the historical acquisition or manufacturing cost (see section 4.3.3.5.1); the estimated period of useful life; as well as the estimated residual value. The useful life is not necessarily the period in which the business asset is economically useful. The latter period may be considerably longer. If at some stage it appears that the useful life is shorter than originally expected, the depreciation percentage must be altered accordingly. The residual value of an asset is the value of the asset at the time it ceases to be of use to the trade or business. The residual value, established at the moment the asset is acquired, remains the same unless there appears to be a considerable change in the residual value which may reasonably be expected to be permanent. Generally, this will be of particular importance in connection with real property.

The most common methods of depreciation are:

- *The straight line method.* In this method annual depreciation is based on a fixed percentage of the acquisition cost, less the estimated residual value. The percentage is established in accordance with the estimated useful life of the asset. This system is generally applied – and for buildings in most cases compulsory – to all depreciable assets.

- *Declining balance method.* In this method the annual depreciation is based on a fixed percentage of the book value. This method cannot be as generally applied as the straight line method; it can only be applied if it can be assumed that the usefulness of the asset in the beginning is considerably higher than in later years. This could, for example, apply to a machine developed to manufacture a product for which there will be a decreasing demand. Assets for which depreciation on book value has also been accepted by the courts include hotels and agricultural buildings.
- Other systems, for example the units of production method, may also be used.

The rules set out above have to be applied in accordance with the provisions laid down in paragraphs 2, 3 and 4 of Article 3.30 and 3.30a ITA 2001. In paragraph 2 of Article 3.30 ITA 2001 is laid down that the annual depreciation of goodwill is maximized to 10% of the acquisition costs. The annual depreciation of other business assets is maximized to 20%. Paragraph 3 of Article 3.30 ITA 2001 provides that intangible assets manufactured by the company itself can be depreciated at once in the year in which they are created. In paragraph 4 of Article 3.30 ITA 2001 is laid down that the costs of business assets with only little value can be depreciated at once.

Article 3.30a ITA contains a special provision with respect to the depreciation of buildings. Apart from the provisions of Article 3.30 ITA 2001 regarding the annual depreciation, depreciation on buildings is only possible if, and when the balance sheet value is higher than its bottom value. The bottom value depends on the Real Estate Tax (WOZ) value which is yearly fixed. A building in use by the owner has a bottom value of 50% of the WOZ value, whereas a building that is meant to be put at the disposal of third parties has a bottom value of 100%.

4.3.3.6 Intangibles

Intangibles such as patents, licenses and goodwill also can be considered to be business assets for tax purposes. In this respect goodwill is the most important in practice. Only purchased goodwill is considered to be a business asset for tax purposes. According to the Supreme Court goodwill is defined as: the profitability of a business exceeding a normal return on the equity and a normal remuneration for the entrepreneur's activities. This profitability is the excess value of all the combined assets, above the aggregate of the assets if each asset were to be valued separately. Purchased goodwill will gradually disappear and, if the profitability is maintained, be replaced by goodwill generated in the business itself. The latter cannot be capitalized but the first may be amortized. As mentioned before, goodwill may be depreciated up to a maximum of 10% yearly.

The costs of other intangibles may be deducted at once if they are manufactured by the company itself.

4.3.3.7 Securities

4.3.3.7.1 General

In valuing securities, a distinction must be made between shares which qualify as a participation for the participation exemption of Article 13 CITA 69, and shares not qualifying as such (a participation of less than 5%) and other securities.

Only the latter two categories will be discussed here. The valuation of participations qualifying for the participation exemption will be discussed in section 4.5.1.

If the securities are listed on a stock exchange, the following valuation systems could be applied:

(a) valuation at cost price;
(b) the price quoted on the stock exchange;
(c) the lower of (a) and (b).

If securities are not listed on a stock exchange, they can be valued at cost price.

4.3.3.7.2 Shareholding in Portfolio Investment Companies

A company which holds 25% or more of the shares in a company that holds mostly portfolio investments (not immovable property) and that is taxed at a rate of less than 10% is obliged to value those shares each year at free-market value (Article 13a CITA 69). However, if the shares would qualify for the participation exemption (which could be the case for insurance companies), then the revaluation does not have to be done.

4.3.4 Valuation of Liabilities

As mentioned under section 4.3.3 (Valuation of Assets) liabilities, if any, must be valued at the balance sheet date. Here again the valuation must be based on the facts existing on the relevant balance sheet date. Facts occurring after the balance sheet date are not taken into consideration, with the exception of those facts which arise from circumstances already in existence on the balance sheet date.

Loans are as a rule valued at face value if they bear normal interest. Interest-free loans – unless short-term – are to be valued at market value. While valuing a loan in the books of the debtor, the question whether he or she can meet his or her obligations is not relevant, so that he or she can still value the loan at face value even if it is obvious that the (full) repayment can never be made.

4.3.4.1 Pensions

With regard to pensions there are basically two possibilities: (1) there are no legal obligations towards the employee but the employer has a strong intention to grant pension rights to the employees; or (2) pension rights have been granted. Consequently a legal obligation exists:

(1) *No legal obligations*: The taxpayer can either choose to deduct the pension payments in the year of payment or alternatively form a reserve, even though theoretically there is no liability but merely a strong intention. Whether an intention exists or not is depending on the circumstances. For instance, there will be no doubt with regard to the intention if the staff has been informed about this intention or if pension payments are made to employees already retired. In fact, if a reserve is formed, this is an equalization reserve as provided for in Article 3.53 paragraph 1 sub a ITA 2001, which is discussed in section 4.4. Such a reserve is used to mitigate the effect of future expenditures by allocating it to the relevant years.

    The fact that the reserve under Article 3.53 paragraph 1 sub a ITA 2001 only recognizes future expenditures prevents the reservation of a lump sum for pensions based on past years (back service). However, these past years can be taken into account by making an annual extra donation in the future by way of recapture.

(2) *Pension rights granted*: There are three possibilities: (i) the pension obligation is provided for in the accounts of the company; (ii) the pensions are issued under a policy with an insurance company; and (iii) the pension obligation is brought under the control of a fund or foundation:

    (i) According to Article 3.29 ITA 2001 a pension reserve has to be valued according to the *capital provision system*. In this system an annual premium is added to a special reserve during the employment years.

        The capital provision is built up by annually calculating the amount to be reserved on the basis of assurance mathematics as stated in Article 3.29 ITA 2001.

    (ii) If the pension policy is issued by an insurance company, the premium must be debited as an expense annually. In case pension rights are granted only after a certain period of employment and also relate to the passed years of employment the premium that has to be paid for those passed years (the back service) can be debited at once. This is the case if the back service must either be paid as a lump sum or must (by way of recapture) be paid in future years as an addition to the premium. In the first case, the amount of the back service can be debited in the year the additional pension obligation is entered into. In the latter case the taxpayer will make a provision in that year. This provision consists of the cash value of the gross premium (i.e. including a margin for expenses). For the purpose of computing the cash value the actual market interest for long-term loans must be used.

    (iii) Where the pension obligation is undertaken by a foundation or pension fund, the system is basically similar to that discussed under (b)(2).

> If the pension fund is one of the large pension funds which insures employees of certain branches, there is no doubt of its independence. This may be different in the case of a foundation or private pension fund, which is in fact fully controlled by the entrepreneur himself or herself. In the latter case the tax authorities will only accept the deduction of pension premiums if they are satisfied that the independence of the foundation or fund is established and the statutory provisions of these entities prevent the possibility of distributions other than pensions being paid.

Finally, it is to be noted that, according to Article 3.27 ITA 2001, in principle expenses or any other charges may not yet be included in the valuation of a pension provision (or any other liability) to the extent that they are influenced by future changes in the price or wages index (coming back service). Expenses or charges relating to these changes can only be debited in the year these changes actually occur or, if it is earlier, in the year the expenses or charges are paid. For pensions, however, an exception has been made; that is, a limited coming back service is accepted under a number of conditions. Briefly speaking, a factor included in a pension premium for future increases in the price or wage index may not exceed 4%.

4.3.5 Business Expenses

4.3.5.1 General

In principle, all the expenses incurred within the scope of the business are deductible for the calculation of the taxable profit. The standard the tax authorities have to apply is whether the expenses are incurred within the scope of the business or for good business reasons. If that is the case, the amount of expenses in principle is immaterial.

4.3.5.2 Expenses Specifically Provided for in CITA 69

In section 4.3.1.4, a reference was made to Article 10 CITA 69 where an enumeration of expenses is given which are not deductible for corporate income tax purposes and which are considered to be distributions. Article 9 CITA 69 gives an illustration – which is again, as follows from the foregoing, a limited illustration – of those expenses which are undoubtedly deductible. Article 9 mentions nine categories in the sections (a) up to and including (i).

In the comment below the paragraphs correspond with the relevant sections of Article 9:

(a) *Profit-related bonuses for the managing director and other staff in respect of their work for the enterprise*. This remuneration is deductible as long as it is not excessive in relation to the work performed. In practice an excessive bonus will only arise in the case of a company controlled by a shareholder who also happens to be the managing director of that company.

(b) *Profit shares paid in respect of concessions, licenses or any other similar performances, such as purchases or deliveries.* These remunerations are deductible provided they are not awarded to persons acting in their capacity as founders, shareholders or other participants.
(c) *Profit shares paid by insurance companies to those insured under a profit-sharing policy.*
(d) *Formation expenses as well as expenses incurred in case of alteration of the statutory capital.*
(e) *The profit share of the managing partners in an open limited partnership.* This only applies to the profit share that the managing partner of an open limited partnership receives in his or her capacity as managing partner. If the managing partner also participates as a limited partner, profit distributions connected therewith are not deductible.
(f) D*eemed interest for government entities* (see also section 4.2.1, under (g)). Government entities may reduce their business income with a fixed percentage of their net assets.
(g) *Profit distributions by a cooperative* or a cooperative foundation out of the annual profit on the basis of the performances – not including capital contributions – by the members. The deductible amount of the profit distributions is, however, restricted; that is, the distribution cannot be deducted to the extent that it exceeds the pro rata part of the total profit of the cooperative which bears the same ratio as the expenses attributable to the performances of the members bear to the total expenses. The amount resulting from this calculation is increased by an amount of EUR 2,269 (2011) but must not exceed the amount of the actual profit.
(h) An entity which focuses exclusively or almost exclusively on the promotion of the public interest or on obtaining funds which, due to a contract, will be distributed to an institution mentioned in Article 16 CITA 69. The expenses with respect to the promotion of the public interest and the funds distributed to the institutions mentioned in Article 16 CITA are deductible unless the deductibility leads to a major distortion of competition.
(i) An entity for the protection of the public interest which is predominantly profitable thanks to the activities of individuals who are not paid or paid below market value, can deduct wages at a level that is at least similar to the statutory minimum wage. This is unless the deductibility leads to a major distortion of competition.

4.3.5.3 Non-Deductible or Partly Deductible Expenses

Certain expenses are not deductible or are only 73.5% deductible.

Not deductible are:

- vessels used for representation purposes;
- fines and penalties imposed by the Netherlands judiciary (including tax fines and penalties); this also applies to fines and penalties imposed by institutions of the EU;

- guns and ammunition unless a legitimization, permission or release is given;
- specific categories of animals unless an animal passport is issued;
- gifts, promises or services if punishable by law (bribes).

If a company has employees, according to the Wages Tax Act 1964, some costs are partially deductible (Article 3.15 ITA 2001). It concerns costs of:

- food, drinks and stimulants (stimulants are: tea, coffee, alcoholic beverages, and so on);
- representation, which covers receptions, parties and entertainment;
- congresses, symposia, seminars, educational trips and the like, including the related travel and lodging.

About 73.5% of these costs are deductible.

With respect to these partly deductible costs a company may opt for full deduction. In that case it has to raise its business income by EUR 4,300 (2011) or, if higher, by 0.4% of the total of annual wages paid to the staff it currently employs.

4.3.5.4 Investment Allowance

The investment allowance is a subsidy on investments in business assets, granted as a deduction from taxable income. There is a general investment allowance, an investment allowance for energy saving assets and an investment allowance for assets that reduce environmental pollution. The deduction that is part of these allowances amounts to a percentage of the amount of money invested in the qualifying assets. In the case of the general investment allowance the percentage declines from 28% for annual investments up to EUR 54,000 to 0% if annual investments are over EUR 301,800 (2011).

If assets for which an investment allowance was obtained are disposed of within five years, the allowance is partially recaptured.

4.3.5.5 Free Depreciation

What was introduced as accelerated depreciation for investments in certain assets which cause fewer environmental pollution and for investments in energy saving assets later on changed into free depreciation. As of 1994 the depreciation for those assets was no longer restricted. Only investments in assets which are specified in a list drawn up by the Minister of Housing, Spatial Planning and the Environment in agreement with the Minister of Finance and the Minister of Economic Affairs qualify for this facility. In order to qualify for the facility, a number of reporting requirements have to be met.

The facility also applies if the qualifying assets are located abroad. In that respect it would make no difference whether the assets are used by the Netherlands investor himself or herself, for example if the assets belong to the assets of a permanent establishment, or if the assets are leased to a non-resident.

4.3.5.6 Ocean Shipping

A taxpayer can request a special way of determining the profit when he or she exploits an ocean vessel. For acceptation of this request a number of conditions have to be met. The request has to be submitted in the first year in which the taxpayer receives profit of ocean shipping.

Profit of ocean shipping is:

- profit through exploitation of a ship intended for the transportation of people or property over international waters or transportation of people or property for the exploration or exploitation of natural wealth at sea;
- profit through exploitation of a ship intended for dredging works at sea which mainly consists of sea transportation or train of barges and assisting activities at sea;
- profit through activities directly linked with the exploitation mentioned above.

When this request is accepted the profit is determined by tonnage.

4.3.5.7 Innovation Box

As of 2007, Article 12b CITA 69 contains the so-called Innovation Box-regime. This Box is meant to give the Netherlands economy a boost. The facility takes the form of a base reduction: the income the box applies to is only partly included in the tax base. This part is based on the formula 5/H, where H stands for the highest percentage of the CIT-rate, that is 25% (year 2011). By this approach, the effective rate for the income the box applies to is only 5%.

The innovation box can only be used if the following conditions are fulfilled:

- the taxpayer has created an intangible;
- the intangible has been patented or is the result from S&O labelled activities (S&O assets);
- the income derived from the intangible is for at least 30% caused by patents granted to the taxpayer or from S&O assets;
- the taxpayer has to comply with additional rules made by regulations. So far these conditions have not been stipulated; and
- a request for the innovation box has to be made.

The innovation box can only be used if the income derived from the intangibles exceeds the production costs of these intangibles. Until that moment, the income is charged by the normal CIT-rate of 25%. From that moment on, the income derived from the intangibles is effectively only charged at 5%.

4.3.5.8 Inter-Company Charges

4.3.5.8.1 General

According to a Supreme Court decision of 1957, the special relationship between a parent company and its subsidiaries has to be disregarded for the purpose of taxation, and where transactions play a part between a parent company and its subsidiaries in the profit calculations of the parent company, such transactions must be compared with transactions with third parties.

Since 2002 Netherlands tax law contains rules with respect to inter-company pricing (Article 8b CITA 69). This article is a codification in the Netherlands tax law of Article 9 of the Organisation for Economic Co-operation and Development (OECD)-model treaty. Companies have to comply with the concept of 'at arm's length' when they are associated. Direct or indirect participation in the management, control or capital of another company leads to association.

The adjustment of prices to an arm's length level is not restricted to transactions between a parent company and its subsidiaries, but also applies to transactions between a shareholder who is a natural persons and his or her company. However, in the latter case the tax authorities will have to show the intention of the parties concerned to set the price at a level which is not at arm's length, whereas transactions between a parent company and its subsidiaries can be adjusted to at arm's length proportions merely because of the fact that they are associated as mentioned in Article 8b CITA 69.

4.3.5.8.2 Tax Treatment of Certain Activities within Multinational Enterprises

The OECD-Member States have made agreements on how to deal with cross-border activities of multinationals. These agreements can be found in the OECD comment of Article 9 OECD-model treaty and in the Transfer Pricing Guidelines for Multinational enterprises and Tax Administrations. The Transfer Pricing Guidelines state methods on how to determine 'arm's length' inter-company prices. These methods can be divided into two categories: traditional transaction methods and transactional profit methods.

The so-called traditional transaction methods for determining transfer prices are based on a comparison of transactions between related parties to transactions between independent enterprises. The following traditional transaction methods can be distinguished:

- Comparable uncontrolled price method (CUP): In this method, an arm's length price is determined by comparison of prices calculated for identical goods, services or property under identical conditions between non-associated parties, called a comparable uncontrolled price. If such free-market transactions can be found, the CUP method is considered to be the most reliable way to determine an arm's length price.

- Resale price method: Under this method, the arm's length price of goods acquired by a taxpayer in a non-arm's length transaction is determined by reducing the price realized on the resale of the goods by the taxpayer to an arm's length party, by an appropriate gross margin and
- Cost plus method: The cost plus method begins with the costs incurred by a supplier of a product or service provided to a non-arm's length enterprise, and a comparable gross mark-up is then added to those costs. In determining the surcharge, the practiced functions of the enterprises involved and the market conditions should be taken into account.

The so-called transactional profit methods are more profit-oriented. In these methods, the achieved profit on a transaction is distributed among the companies involved in that transaction. The following transactional profit methods can be distinguished:

- Profit split method: In this method, firstly there has to be determined how much profit would have been made on a transaction if this transaction had taken place between non-associated parties. Then, this profit must be attributed to the companies involved in an economically acceptable manner, so that an arm's length result is approached. In attributing the profit, the position of the companies involved has to be taken into account; and
- Transactional net margin method: This method compares the net profit margin of a taxpayer arising from a non-arm's length transaction with the net profit margins realized by arm's length parties from similar transactions and examines the net profit margin relative to an appropriate base such as costs, sales or assets.

To show that they have acted at arm's length, associated companies have to include data in their records showing how transfer prices have been established and from which can be concluded that these conditions would have been agreed by independent parties. In Dutch tax law, this documentation requirement is laid down in Article 8b, CITA 69. If a tax payer fails to fulfil this obligation, he or she must show that an arm's length price has been agreed when there is a dispute with the tax inspector (*reverse burden of proof*).

4.3.5.8.3 Deductibility of Interest Payments

In determination of the taxable profit, interest paid to the provider of a loan can be deducted. Laid down by law as well as determined in jurisprudence, deduction of interest can sometimes be limited or prohibited.

Article 10a CITA 69 states, that interest paid to an associated enterprise or person is not deductible when the underlying debt is related to one of the following legal acts:

- a profit distribution or refund of paid-up capital;
- a capital contribution;
- an acquisition or expansion of a participation in another company.

As of 1 January 2008, a deviation of the above non-deductibility is possible when the tax payer can prove it is plausible that:

- the legal act and the debt are predominantly motivated by business considerations;
- the creditor is confronted with a compensating tax charge on the received interest of at least 10%. This condition is not fulfilled if the tax inspector can prove that the debt is entered into by the creditor in order to set-off the received interest against losses suffered by the creditor. There is no compensating tax charge either if the inspector can prove that the legal act and the debt are not predominantly motivated by business considerations. The latter exception applies even if the tax rate is at least 10%.

Interest can also be not deductible with respect to a debt between associated parties that has no fixed repayment schedule or will have to be repaid only after more than 10 years. This is the case when no interest is charged on the loan or if the interest charged on the loan is clearly lower than an arm's length interest. Article 10b CITA 69 does not only forbids the deduction of interest but also the change in value op the debt is non-deductible when the interest is considerably below market value.

Article 10d CITA 69 aims at preventing excessive financing with debts within a concern thin capitalization). This Article was entered into force after the Bosal judgment of 18 September 2003. The legislator had to remove an article that limited deduction of costs made in connection with foreign participations. Without countermeasures the legislator was afraid of tax base erosion because of thin capitalization. Article 10d CITA 69 determines that interest paid to an associated enterprise is not deductible if the debt equity ratio of a company is above a certain level. In that case the interest that corresponds with the excessive part of the debt burden is not deductible. Article 10d CITA 69 will only be applied if a company is part of a group and the amount of non-deductible interest will never be more that the interest paid to other group companies.

4.3.5.8.4 Conduit Companies

Article 8c CITA 69 was entered into force as of 1 January 2002. This article applies to conduit companies that operate without significant risk. In that case the interest paid to and by these companies as well as the royalties paid to and by these companies are ignored when computing the tax base. Consequently the conduit company cannot set-off (foreign) withholding tax on received interest and royalties with Netherlands CIT. This does not mean that a conduit company is not taxed if Article 8c CITA 69 is applied. It will be taxed for the services it offers while its profit is calculated on the basis of arm's length prices.

4.4 TAX-FREE RESERVES

The term reserves is often confused with other items on the credit side of the balance sheet. This primarily involves provisions and accrued liabilities. Before explaining the tax-free reserves, a short description of provisions and accrued liabilities will be added.

Provisions: a future expense or loss which has not materialized yet but is related to the present year. A legally enforceable obligation is not a provision. Provisions are a part of the loan capital. A contribution to a provision is charged to the profit of the enterprise.

Accrued liabilities: amounts that, after closing the balance sheet of the related year, should be paid in a posterior year. Also income received in advance relating to a subsequent financial year is included.

Reserves: amounts put aside from the profit with respect to future expenses. Contributions to fiscal reserves are deductible from the profit of the taxpayer. The reserves are part of the equity of the company. Article 3.53 ITA 2001 provides for three types of tax-free reserves:

- equalization reserve (Article 3.53 ITA 2001);
- reinvestment reserve (Article 3.54 ITA 2001);
- retirement reserve (Article 3.67–3.73 ITA 2001).

The retirement reserve is not permitted for corporate income tax.

4.4.1 Equalization Reserves

Sometimes certain expenses are effectively incurred in the future whereas a proper allocation would mean that they should be deducted in earlier years. The tax legislation has recognized this possibility and therefore allowed an equalization reserve so that the effect of this future expenditure may be mitigated and a proper allocation of the costs can be realized. In practice, the reserve is used mainly for maintenance costs. The most common example is the survey reserve for ships which must be thoroughly surveyed periodically, but it could also apply to pensions in those cases where the employer has not yet entered into an obligation to grant pension rights but merely has an intention to do so. Whether or not such an intention exists should be proved by reasonable evidence (see also section 4.3.4.1.

An equalization reserve can be started in any tax year. However, Article 3.53 ITA 2001 only recognizes future expenditures. It is not possible to make a reservation of a lump sum for past years. These past years can be taken into account by making an annual extra donation in the future by way of recapture. The equalization reserve expires:

- by charging the expenses actually incurred;
- if it is obvious that the purpose for which the reserve had been created no longer exists;
- if the taxpayer has ceased to maintain regular book-keeping;
- if the company ceases to be a payer.

The reserve is restricted to specific future costs and may not be used for future investments such as the purchase of a new capital asset. When it turns out that the equalization reserve is higher than the costs the exceeding amount has to be added to the profit.

4.4.2 Reinvestment Reserve

Where a tangible or intangible business asset (with the exception of intangible fixed assets held as a portfolio investment) is either sold at a gain or damaged, and the proceeds from the insurance exceed the cost price, the taxation of the gain may be deferred by creating a so-called reinvestment reserve. The reinvestment reserve is not obligatory. Consequently, it may be used for one asset but not for another. The reserve can only be formed if and as long the taxpayer has the intention to reinvest in new assets. The required reinvestment should not occur later than three years after the year in which the reserve was formed, unless there are special circumstances for the delay and measures to replace have already been started. If no reinvestment occurred within the three-year period, the original gain will be added to the taxable profit and taxed at the ordinary rate. This may also occur at an earlier stage if the intention to reinvest no longer exists.

Not every asset qualifies for reinvestment. In case the sold or damaged asset (the original asset) is not depreciated or depreciated during a period of more than 10 years, the new asset must be of a similar nature as the original asset; that is, it should have a similar economic function within the enterprise. This must be interpreted in a broad sense.

There are two additional requirements: the reinvestment reserve has to be deducted from the cost price of the acquired asset so that future depreciation will be lower. Furthermore, the costs price of the acquired asset may not be lower than the book value of the original asset when sold or damaged. If so, the difference will be added to the taxable profit in the year of reinvestment.

4.5 EXEMPTIONS

There are a number of exemptions provided for in the income tax and corporate income tax legislation. Some of them are provided for in Articles 3.11, 3.12 and 3.13 ITA 2001, but also apply to the corporate taxpayer. There is, however, an exemption which applies to corporate taxpayers only. This is the participation exemption.

4.5.1 Participation Exemption

4.5.1.1 Introduction

The Business Tax Act of 1893 already provided for a participation exemption with respect to dividends. Although there have been changes, the basic principle has been maintained over the years. The CITA 69 decreased the shareholding requirement from 25% to 5%, and the exemption was extended to capital gains.

The participation exemption has been introduced to avoid double taxation of profits. The exemption applies to all corporate taxpayers (see the enumeration in section 4.2.1), except certain portfolio investment companies. The exemption also applies to qualifying holdings in foreign companies.

Companies are exempt from corporate income tax on all 'benefits' connected with a qualifying shareholding. The so-called participation exemption provisions do not only cover cash dividends but also stock dividends, bonus shares, dividends in kind, hidden profit distributions, foreign exchange gains realized on the shares as such in a foreign subsidiary and capital gains realized upon the disposal of a shareholding. Capital losses on the shareholding are not tax deductible, except in the case of liquidation of the subsidiary concerned. However, the deductibility of a loss upon liquidation of a subsidiary is restricted.

4.5.1.2 Application of the Participation Exemption or Participation Credit

4.5.1.2.1 Participations

For qualifying participations the taxpayer is legally entitled to the participation exemption. No request is needed. The participation exemption excludes benefits of the participation from the tax base. For so-called 'non-qualifying investment participations' the taxpayer is not entitled to the participation exemption, but only to a participation credit. The participation credit offers a tax credit for benefits out of these non-qualifying investment participations.

The following condition must be met in order to qualify as a participation. There must be at least a 5% shareholding (of the nominal paid-up capital of the company; a company whose capital is divided into shares). A membership of a cooperation or a cooperative society and ownership of at least 5% of the participation certificates of an investment association also qualify. Both legal and economic ownership qualifies. Exceptionally, a shareholding of less than 5% sometimes qualifies as a participation. This is the case in Article 13 sub 5 and sub 16 CITA 69.

The participation exemption also applies to foreign subsidiaries. For instance: a Belgium SA or Bvba, a German AG or GmbH, a French SA or SARL and an Italian SPA or SARL. The Supreme Council decided that an LLC (Limited Liability Company), established under the law of the American state Delaware, can also be a participation. The LLC was judged to be similar to a subsidiary whose capital is divided into shares.

4.5.1.2.2 Investment Participations

As mentioned, under circumstances, the taxpayer is not entitled to the participation exemption with regard to (domestic and foreign) investment participations. A company qualifies as an investment participation when the taxpayer holds his or her shares:

- in line with normal portfolio investment management; or
- in a subsidiary whose activities consist of having investments; or
- in a subsidiary that is fictitious investment participation (which is usually the case when the assets of the participation consist for more than 50% of interests less than 5% in other companies or when the activities of the participation consist for more than 50% of financing group companies).

For the participation in investment participations the taxpayer is only entitled to the participation exemption when the investment participation is a so-called 'qualifying investment participation'. This is the case if:

- the investment participation is liable to an effective tax burden of at least 10%; and/or
- the assets of the participation consist for less than 50% of free investments. Free investments are investments that are not related to a business that is otherwise carried out by the participation. Real estate is not considered to be a free investment unless the participation is taxed on the basis of Article 28 CIT.

When a participation is an investment participation but does not meet one of the latter conditions, the investment participation is a so-called 'non-qualifying investment participation'. In that case the taxpayer is not entitled to the participation exemption with regard to that participation, but only to the participation credit. This means that the gross dividend is fully taxed at the taxpayers' level. However, the tax burden will be lowered by a credit (which is an estimate of the tax paid by the participation (5%)). In the end the effective tax burden on the dividend (the tax due by the shareholder together with the tax due by the investment participation) therefore usually will be equal to the Netherlands CIT-rate. The credit system for non-qualifying investment participations aims at preventing the departure of group financing activities and portfolio investments to tax havens.

4.5.1.3 Expenses Connected with a Participation

Expenses related to a qualifying participation cannot always be deducted. Acquisition costs as well as selling costs related to the participation, for example notarial charges, exchange duties, purchase and selling commissions, are not deductible. However, so-called day-to-day costs are deductible, for example financing and maintenance costs of the subsidiary, costs of collecting dividends, storage charges. With financing costs are included the interest and closing costs due on the loan with which the purchase of the participation is financed. Currency exchange losses on loans which are used to acquire a foreign participation are tax deductible, according to a 1977 Netherlands Supreme Court decision. However, the parent company may opt for applying the exemption to all currency exchange profits and losses on loans related to foreign participations.

In contrast with participations that qualify for the participation exemption, costs related to non-qualifying investment participations are deductible.

4.5.1.4 Participation Exemption and Written Off Receivables

Article 13b CITA 69 states that a taxpayer (parent company) that has written off a receivable held in a subsidiary is obliged to add to its taxable profit an amount equal to the amount of the write off if this receivable:

- is sold to a company associated with the parent company;
- is transferred to a foreign permanent establishment;
- if the business of the subsidiary is fully or partially transferred to the parent company or a company associated with the parent company.

On selling the receivable or the business to a company resident abroad, the acquiring company is deemed to be associated with the parent company, unless the parent company can demonstrate otherwise.

Article 13ba CITA 69 is another provision with respect to a taxpayer (parent company) that has written off a receivable held in a subsidiary. He or she is obliged to add to its taxable profit an amount equal to the amount of the write off if the receivable:

- is used to pay up new shares in the subsidiary in question;
- is adjusted in such a way that it is considered similar to equity and the parent company is entitled to participation exemption with respect to the receivable;
- is waived, if and to the extent that such waiver has not resulted in taxable profit with the subsidiary.

However, the taxpayer can choose to allocate the write off that he or she has to add to his or her taxable profit to a revaluation reserve (*opwaarderingsreserve*). Consequently, no tax is levied yet. The revaluation reserve has to be added to the taxable profit as the value of the participation in the subsidiary increases. Under some circumstances, the revaluation reserve can be (partly) dissolved tax-free. The most important situation is when the taxpayer sells the shares in the subsidiary to a not related party.

4.5.1.5 Conversion of a Permanent Establishment into a Subsidiary

If a foreign permanent establishment is converted into a subsidiary, the participation exemption will not apply to the profits resulting from this participation until the permanent establishment's remaining losses, if any, from the previous years have been recovered (Article 13c CITA 69). There are several provisions which prevent abuse of the above principle by, for instance, transferring the participation to a foreign company or transferring the participation's business activities.

4.5.1.6 Liquidation Losses

As indicated earlier, there is one exception to the rule that negative benefits from participation are not tax deductible. This is when a (Netherlands or foreign) participation is liquidated and a liquidation loss (if any) results. This loss is tax deductible from the fiscal profit of the parent company (Article 13d CITA 69).

In this respect it should be noted, however, that a legal merger, as result of which a company as well as the share capital issued by that company cease to exist, cannot be considered a liquidation, according to a decision of the Netherlands Supreme Court in 1990. Therefore, a loss suffered on a participation as a result of a legal merger is not tax deductible.

4.5.1.6.1 The Size of the Liquidation Loss

Liquidation losses are fixed at the amount by which the cost price of the participation exceeds the total liquidation distribution.

Profits (dividends) derived from the participation during the five years preceding the year in which the participation suspends its business activities (in some cases in the 10 preceding years) must also be included in the computation of the liquidation distribution.

4.5.1.6.2 Liquidation of Intermediate Holding Companies

If a dissolved company's net assets included a participation which:

- is part of the liquidation distribution; or
- has been sold;

and which has decreased in value since the acquisition of the participation in the dissolved company, the liquidation loss may only be taken into account if and to the extent it exceeds the decrease in value (of the participation held by the dissolved company).

Article 13d CITA 69 provides no specific definition of the term 'intermediate holding company'. Each subsidiary which has (or has had) a participation in another company is therefore an intermediate holding company.

4.5.1.6.3 The Date on Which the Liquidation Loss May Be Taken into Account

The liquidation loss will be taken into account on the date on which the liquidation is complete.

Furthermore, the following conditions must be met:

(1) The parent company and companies with which it is associated and – if so – the entity which continues the business activities of the dissolved

company may not otherwise be entitled to obtain tax relief for losses which could not be offset by the liquidated subsidiary.

(2) The business activities of the dissolved company must:
  - be completely suspended; or
  - be fully or partially continued by a company other than the parent company or any of its associated companies.

Under certain circumstances, the loss excluded on the grounds of this condition can still be carried forward and set-off at a later date.

According to a 2010 ruling of the Netherlands Under Minister of Finance, if a subsidiary has gone bankrupt or into liquidation and the company has not been dissolved within eight years after the adjudication order or within eight years after the decision to liquidate the company, then a liquidation loss, if any, can generally be taken into account in the eighth year.

4.5.2 The Forestry Exemption

Profits derived from an enterprise involved in the exploitation of forests is exempt from taxation. The sale of underbrush is not included. The question what constitutes a forest enterprise has been extensively interpreted by the court. A disadvantage of the fact that profits from a forest enterprise are exempt is that on the other hand losses derived from this activity – which will generally be the case – cannot be deducted from other profits or income. Therefore, the law provides for a possibility for the taxpayer to waive this exemption.

4.5.3 Agricultural Exemption

The second exemption concerns profits derived from an agricultural enterprise which can be allocated to changes in the value of the land. An agricultural enterprise includes raising cattle, growing plants and flowers, as well as fresh-water fishing.

4.5.4 Remission of Debts

As a general rule remission of debts for business reasons – debts belonging to the assets of an enterprise – will result in a taxable profit for the debtor. There is one exception, however. Profits arising from the remission of business debts which cannot be collected, for instance because there are no longer any assets, are not taxable to the extent that they exceed the company's tax losses. It follows that although the profit arising from the remission is exempt it does absorb losses, if any, available for compensation.

4.6 CHARITABLE DONATIONS

The CITA specifically provides for a deduction of charitable gifts. In most cases donations by a company will be deductible expenses; that is, if other considerations such as advertising promotion have prompted the gift rather than charity.

Article 16 CITA 69 provides for a deduction where gifts are made to public benefit institutions, mentioned in Article 6.33 ITA 2001 (the so-called *ANBI's*). The deduction is allowed to the extent that the gifts in total exceed EUR 227 and to a maximum of 10% of the profit.

Gifts are defined as benefits extended out of generosity and non-obligatory contributions but only insofar as no rights which can be valued in cash arise through the gifts.

4.7 LOSS RELIEF

4.7.1 Introduction

As of 1 January 2007, there is a one-year carry-back and a nine year carry-forward period. For the purpose of setting-off, a loss must follow the sequence in which the loss was incurred. Thus, losses are to be set-off against the oldest year. A loss is defined as a negative profit.

4.7.2 Losses of Inactive Companies

There are some restrictions on loss relief for the so-called inactive company. Article 20a, CITA 69 determines that losses can no longer be carried forward if, since the beginning of the earliest year for which a loss must be offset against the current year the ultimate participants in an inactive company have significantly (30% or more) changed. This rule applies to all losses that have been incurred for the moment when the 30% or more change has taken effect. Not all changes in the ultimate participants give rise to the application of Article 20a CITA 69. The article shall not apply with respect to modifications: (a) resulting from changes incurred by inheritance or matrimony, or (b) relating to an increase of an already existing participation of at least one-third in the inactive company at the beginning of the earliest year, mentioned above. Further exceptions are to be found in Article 20a CITA 69. If a taxpayer wants certainty about whether or not Article 20a CITA 69 is applicable he or she may inquire with the inspector. The inspectors' decision will be eligible for objection.

4.8 FISCAL UNITY

4.8.1 INTRODUCTION

According to Article 15 up to and including 15aj and 15a CITA 69, a parent company and its (at least 95%) subsidiary can be combined into a so-called fiscal unity and file a consolidated return.

The fiscal unity is recognized for corporate income tax purposes only. Legally all entities involved remain separate entities. Once fiscal unity is obtained it does not have to be applied indefinitely. The unity may be terminated (partly) after one or more years. Thereafter, the members of the former unity will become taxable separately. Within a fiscal unity, assets and liabilities, profits and losses are deemed to be owned, earned or incurred by the parent company. A fiscal unity is only applied at the request of the companies involved. As long as the conditions for the application are met, such a request will be approved. The unity does not apply to all the subsidiaries of a parent, but only to those subsidiaries for which a request has been made. The advantages of a fiscal unity include: the setting-off of losses among unity members and any transfer of assets within the unity can be affected at book value. This also provides for the possibility to tax-free reorganizations.

There are, however, also disadvantages due to the various conditions which are imposed to prevent abuse.

4.8.2 CONDITIONS IMPOSED BY LAW

The following seven conditions are imposed with respect to the claiming of fiscal unity:

(1) the parent must be an NV, a BV, a mutual insurance company or a cooperative association formed under Netherlands law. The subsidiary must be an NV or BV. For both parent and subsidiary applies that the following legal persons can also be part of fiscal unity: legal persons established under the law of the BES-Islands, Curaçao, Aruba, Saint Martin, Member States of the EU, or a State with which the Netherlands have concluded a tax treaty for the prevention of double taxation, in which there is a provision that prohibits discrimination on grounds of nationality for tax payers in the same circumstances as those set up under Netherlands law. These tax payers must be similar to the above listed legal persons that are established under Netherlands law (see Article 15, subparagraph 3d CITA 69);

(2) the participating companies must be established in the Netherlands;
(3) the parent must own, legally as well as beneficially, all or at least 95% of the shares of the subsidiary company;
(4) parent and subsidiary must have the same financial year;
(5) for the determination of profit all companies must apply the same provisions, unless the Minister of Finance provides otherwise;
(6) the shares in the subsidiary must not be held as inventory; and
(7) parent and subsidiary(ies) have to make a joint request for fiscal unity.

In 1994, the Netherlands Supreme Court held that a subsidiary, which was resident in the Netherlands but which was not formed under Netherlands law, could nevertheless be part of a fiscal unity. The case involved an NV formed under the laws of the Netherlands Antilles, with its place of effective management located in the Netherlands. The Supreme Court based its decision on Article 1, paragraph 1 of the law regulating fiscal matters within the Kingdom of the Netherlands. According to this provision, entities not established under domestic law shall not be subject in the Netherlands, the Netherlands Antilles and Aruba to any taxation or any requirement connected therewith which is more burdensome than that to which Netherlands nationals or, as the case may be, entities established under domestic law are subject to in the same circumstances. According to the Supreme Court, an Antilles NV had the same or almost the same characteristics as a Netherlands NV. Therefore, the Antilles NV was allowed to form part of a fiscal unity. Following this judgment Article 15, third paragraphs c and d, CITA 69 has been adapted.

4.8.3 The Beginning and Dissolution of the Fiscal Unity

Article 15aa CITA 69 defines the moment from which a taxable person will be treated as part of a fiscal unity. Article 15(5), CITA 69 then indicates that a fiscal unity is established on the date the taxpayers choose, but no earlier than three months for the submission of the request for fiscal unity. Finally a fiscal unity cannot be formed before all requirements, with the exception of the request, of a fiscal entity have been complied with. Thus, when the requirements for fiscal unity are met, the taxpayers have three months time to request for fiscal unity and so fiscal unity starts at the date on which the requirements are met.

The end of a fiscal unity can have multiple causes. According to Article 15 (6) CITA 69 a fiscal unity ends:

- if the requirements for fiscal unity are no longer met (paragraph 6, subparagraph (a);
- if a foreign taxpayer whose Netherlands permanent establishment is part of fiscal unity becomes resident of the Netherlands (paragraph 6, subparagraph (b));
- if a Netherlands taxpayer emigrates leaving behind a permanent establishment in the Netherlands (paragraph 6 of part c); or
- at the joint request of the parent and subsidiary(ies) (paragraph 6, part d).

4.9 MERGERS AND REORGANIZATIONS

4.9.1 General Observations

There are, in fact, three types of merger. They can be separated into two main groups. Firstly, the contractual merger format and, secondly, the legal merger format. Two options of the contractual format are the stock merger and the business merger. In this form of merger, the merging companies retain their own legal status. This in contrast to a legal merger. In that case the merging companies amalgamate together. Since 15 July 2008 there is a possibility for a cross-border legal merger. A cross-border legal merger offers a Netherlands NV, BV or a European cooperative company the possibility of merging with a capital company or cooperative company established under the law of another Member State of the EU or the European economic area.

4.9.2 Stock Merger

In case of a stock merger, the shareholders of a company assign their stock over to another company (the acquiring company). The contracting partners are the acquiring company and the shareholders of the acquired company. The acquiring company can be an existing or a newly created company. Payment can be done by way of cash or by issuing shares in the acquiring company. The merger could result in an income tax liability for the individual shareholders transferring their shares, provided they had a substantial interest in the transferee company. However, there are some roll over provisions. These provisions are described in Article 3.55 ITA 2001. In case the shareholder is a company subjected to CIT Article 3.55 ITA 2001 is also applicable unless the company is entitled to the participation exemption (Article 13 CITA 69). In the latter case no tax is due with respect to the transfer of the shares and there is no need for the roll over provision of Article 3.55 ITA 2001.

4.9.3 Merger by Way of a Transfer of Assets and Liabilities (Company Merger)

A company merger can be effected through a sale of an enterprise or a substantive part thereof either for cash or for shares. Without the application of special provisions, the transferring company would be liable to tax on any gain resulting from the difference between the actual consideration and the tax book value of the assets and the liabilities transferred. If the consideration consists of cash, the payment of corporation tax will generally not be a problem. If the consideration consists of shares, the imposition of tax may be a serious obstacle. Consequently, Article 14 CITA 69 provides for a tax exempt merger which only applies if the conditions laid down in this article are met. An over all condition is that the company merger may not have as its main objective the evasion or undue delay of corporate tax. Further conditions are laid down in paragraph 1 of Article 14 CIT (the company merger without conditional approval) and in paragraph 2 of Article 14 CIT (the company merger with conditional approval of the tax authorities).

4.9.3.1 Company Merger without Conditional Approval

A company merger, provided for in Article 14, paragraph 1, CITA 69, applies if the following conditions are met:

(a) there is a transfer of an enterprise or a separate part of an enterprise;
(b) the acquirer issues shares in return for the transferred enterprise;
(c) the transferor and acquirer are subject to the same profit regime;
(d) the acquirer is not entitled to the carry-forward of losses;
(e) the acquirer is not entitled to a roll over reduction because of double taxation in respect of foreign results;
(f) the acquirer is not entitled to the innovation box;
(g) the acquirer is not entitled to a roll over reduction of the participation credit; and
(h) subsequent taxation with respect to the exempted profit is assured.

4.9.3.2 Company Merger with Conditional Approval of Tax Authorities

If a company merger cannot be achieved under the conditions referred to in Article 14, paragraph 1, CITA 69, which are summarized above in section 4.9.3.1, the company merger exemption only applies upon request if the approval of the tax authorities is acquired. The request has to be submitted to the tax inspector prior to the merger. The approval may be refused. The Department of Finance has by way of a model issued standard conditions that have to be met by the transferor and the acquirer.

If the exemption is refused, or if the taxpayers do not agree with the conditions imposed, the tax payer can appeal by going to the Tax Court and (ultimately) the Supreme Court.

4.9.4 Legal Merger

In case of a legal merger two or more legal persons (companies) merge into another acquiring company or in a newly created company. A legal merger is a transfer for the company that ceases to exist (the dissolved company). Moreover, shareholders and creditors of the dissolved company are supposed to dispose of their shares, loans and advances to the dissolved company.

For the dissolved company Article 14b CITA 69 provides for a tax-exempt transfer under the imposition of a number of conditions. The main condition is that the legal merger is not predominantly focused on the evasion or the undue deferral of taxation. Another condition is that the tax book value of the transferred assets and liabilities of the dissolved company are continued by the acquiring company. In this way the tax claim on the exempted profit is rolled over to the latter company.

If the requirements of Article 14b (2) CITA 69 are met, the dissolved company is entitled to a tax-exempt legal merger without the intervention of the Inspector. The requirements in question are as follows:

- the dissolved company and the acquiring company must be subject to the same profit regime;
- neither the dissolved company nor the acquiring company has the right to carry-forward losses;
- the dissolved company nor the acquiring company has a right to a roll over reduction that prevents double taxation in respect of foreign results;
- the dissolved company and the acquiring company are not entitled to the innovation box;
- the dissolved company nor the acquiring company are entitled to a roll over reduction of the participation credit; and
- subsequent taxation with respect to the exempted profit is assured.

4.9.5 Legal Division

Division is the opposite of a merger. Division is defined as an operation whereby a company, on being dissolved without going into liquidation, transfers all its assets and liabilities to two or more existing or new companies, in exchange for the pro rata issue to its shareholder of securities representing the capital of the companies receiving the assets and liabilities, and, if applicable, a cash payment not exceeding 10% of the nominal value or, in absence of a nominal value, of the accounting par value of those securities. Another type of legal division is the so-called 'partial division'. This is defined as an operation whereby a company transfers, without being dissolved, one or more branches of activity, to one or more existing or new companies, leaving at least one branch of activity in the transferring company.

Article 14a CITA 69 states that the transferring company has fictitiously sold the transferred assets. The profit made in respect of the division is consequently taxed. However, Article 14a CITA 69 under certain conditions provides for a tax-exempt legal division. A tax-exempt legal division is only possible if the legal division is not predominantly focused on the evasion or deferral of taxation. Furthermore, the conditions of Article 14a(2) have to be fulfilled. These conditions correspond to the conditions of Article 14b(2) CITA 69, see section 4.9.4. If one or more of the conditions are not fulfilled, a tax-exempt legal division can only take place upon request with the approval of the tax authorities.

4.10 INVESTMENT INSTITUTIONS

4.10.1 General Introduction

There are two special tax regimes for investment institutions. The first regime is referred to as the Exempt Investment Institution regime (VBI; Article 6a CITA 69). The second regime is referred to as the Fiscal Investment Institution regime (FBI; Article 28 CITA 69).

4.10.2 Exempt Investment Institution

4.10.2.1 Introduction

An investment institution as meant in Article 1:1 of the Act on Financial Supervision is on request exempt from corporate income tax, provided the conditions of Article 6a of the Dutch Corporate Tax Act are met (exempt investment institution).

4.10.2.2 Conditions

A company qualifies as an exempt investment institution if the following conditions are met:

(a) the statutory as well as the actual objective of the corporation is the investment of cash and other assets;
(b) the corporation invests solely in financial instruments as in Article 1:1 of the Act on the Financial Supervision and in savings, and operates in accordance with the principle of risk-diversification;
(c) the shares of the corporation are on request of the shareholders issued or redeemed directly or indirectly out of the corporation's assets (open-end investment institution);
(d) the investment institution concerns an under Dutch law incorporated public company (NV) or an under Dutch law established investment association (*fonds voor gemene rekening*) or a company incorporated or established under the law of a BES Island, as well as the law of Aruba, Curaçao, Sint Maarten, a Member State of the EU or a state which has entered into a tax treaty with the Netherlands that includes a non-discrimination clause for corporations, but only if the company is comparable to one of the aforementioned under Dutch law incorporated or established companies.

4.10.2.3 Creation of an Exempt Investment Institution

An already existing corporation subject to the regular corporate income tax or a fiscal investment institution (see section 4.10.3) can acquire the status of exempt investment institution as of the beginning of the year following the year in which all the requirements are met. From then on the company will be exempt from corporate income tax. In this prior year a final tax calculation must be made. The difference between the book value and the market value of the assets will be added to the taxable profit, as well as the fiscal reserves.

A newly incorporated company or established investment association can apply for the status of exempt investment institution from the date of incorporation, provided it meets the requirements mentioned in section 4.11.2.

4.10.2.4 Taxation of Shareholders

The Act on Financial Supervision does not lay down whether the profit earned by an exempt investment institution has to be distributed or not. The latter is therefore determined by the fund rules. In order to prevent that the income is not subject to tax until the disposal of the shares in a tax-exempt investment institution, company shareholders – shareholders other than private investors or exempt entities – have to revalue their shares continuously at market value. As a result, any change in value of the shares in the exempt investment institution is taxed in the hands of these shareholders.

4.10.2.5 Foreign Withholding Taxes and Tax Treaty Eligibility

An exempt investment institution is subjectively exempt. Hence, it cannot rely on the Tax Charter for the Kingdom of the Netherlands, the Netherlands tax treaties and unilateral rules for the crediting of dividend withholding tax or foreign withholding tax. The Corporate Tax Act does not provide for any other relief for the withholding tax levied by a source state on income that is derived from an underlying investment. Nor are the shareholders of these companies under the Netherlands ITA or Corporate Tax Act allowed to credit the foreign withholding tax as if they had invested directly.

The Ministry of Finance has recently stated that the Netherlands will make an effort with tax treaty partners to regard exempt investment institutions as tax treaty eligible. It is, however, prepared to agree with its tax treaty partners on the exclusion of some tax treaty benefits, like the application of a reduced tax rate or an exemption from withholding tax on dividends or interest in the state of the treaty partner. It is therefore doubtful whether this effort will make it easier for exempt investment institutions claiming tax treaty benefits (see for more information *Notitie Fiscaal Verdragsbeleid 2011*).

4.10.3 Fiscal Investment Institution

4.10.3.1 General Introduction

An under Dutch law incorporated public company (NV including a *SE*), an under Dutch law incorporated private company with limited liability (BV) or an under

Dutch law established investment association (*fonds voor gemene rekening*) may under a number of conditions qualify for the special tax status provided for in Article 28 of the Corporate Tax Act and the Investment Institutions Decree of 1970 (as amended later on). The regime for fiscal investments institution is also open for corporations incorporated or established under the law of a BES Island, as well as the law of Aruba, Curaçao, Sint Maarten, a Member State of the EU or a state which has enclosed a tax treaty with the Netherlands that includes a non-discrimination clause for corporations, but only if they are comparable to one of the above-mentioned under Dutch law incorporated or established corporations.

The fiscal investment institution is subject to corporate income tax although at a tax rate of nil per cent, provided a number of conditions are met. The concept of fiscal investment institutions aims to avoid double taxation. The basic idea is that it should not make a difference whether an investor invests directly or by way of a fiscal investment institution.

4.10.3.2 Conditions

A company qualifies as a fiscal investment institution if the following conditions are met:

(a) the statutory as well as the actual objective of the corporation must be the investment of assets;
(b) the loans obtained, if any, may only consist of:
  - loans on real estate, not exceeding 60% of the book value of the immovable property;
  - any other loans not exceeding 20% of the book value of the other investments.
(c) within eight months after the end of the book year the fiscal profit must be distributed to the shareholders (or in the case of an investment association to the participants);
(d) if the shares (or in the case of an investment association: the participations) in the fiscal investment institution are authorized to be traded on a market on financial instruments as meant in Article 1:1 of the Act on Financial Supervision, or a fiscal investment institution or its management company has an authorization meant in Article 2:65 of the Act on Financial Supervision or is exempt from such authorization on the basis of Article 2:66 of the Act on Financial Supervision, 45% or more of its stock may not be held by one company or by associated companies (parent company, subsidiary and sister companies with an interest of at least one-third) which are subject to corporate income tax at the regular rate, whereas an individual may not have an interest of 25% or more.
(e) if the shares (or in the case of an investment association the participations) in the fiscal investment institution are not authorized to be traded on a market on financial instruments as meant in Article 1:1 of the Act on Financial Supervision, or a fiscal investment institution or its management

company does not have an authorization on the basis of Article 2:65 of the Act on Financial Supervision or is not exempt from such an authorization on the basis of Article 2:66 of the Act on Financial Supervision, at least 75% of the shares (or in the case of an investment association the participations) must be kept by individuals, and/or companies not subject to or exempt from corporate income tax and/or fiscal investment institutions as meant in sub (d), while an individual may not have a qualifying interest in the fiscal investment institution as meant in section 4.3 of the ITA 2001.

(f) the profit of the fiscal investment institution must be distributed equally on all shares;

(g) residents of the Netherlands or Netherlands corporations may not own 25% or more of the shares in the fiscal investment institution through non-resident corporations or non-resident investment funds;

(h) in the case of a fiscal investment institution as meant in (d) the directors as well as half of the members of the supervisory board may not be a director or a member of the supervisory board of another company which has an interest of 25% or more in the fiscal investment institution, unless the other company is a fiscal investment institution as meant in (d).

4.10.3.3 Creation of a Fiscal Investment Institution

An already existing corporation subject to the normal corporate income tax can acquire the status of fiscal investment institution as of the beginning of the year following the year in which all the requirements are met. From then on the company will be subject to a nil per cent corporate income tax rate. In the last year before acquiring the status of fiscal investment institution a final tax calculation must be made. The difference between the book value and the market value of the assets will be added to the taxable profit, as well as the fiscal reserves.

Where a newly incorporated company or established investment association would apply for the fiscal investment institution status it can be treated as such from the date of incorporation, provided it meets the requirements mentioned in section 4.10.2. Nevertheless, the State Secretary for Finance has granted a temporary exemption from some of these conditions. The exemption, however, expires not later than 24 months after incorporation.

4.10.3.4 Calculation of Profit; Special Reserves

For the calculation of the profit for tax purposes, the same rules apply as to any other entity subject to corporate income tax. There are, however, some exceptions. For example, the participation exemption does not apply. Nor does the Parent-Subsidiary Directive.

On the other hand, the fiscal investment institution can benefit from two special reserves: the so-called reinvestment account and the round-off reserve. The first one is the most important. Both are typical for fiscal investment institutions.

(a) *The reinvestment* account: Capital gains are included in the fiscal profit so that without any special measures they would have to be distributed. A fiscal investment institution may, however, decide to reserve such profits in a reinvestment account and hence avoid distribution. The choice for the creation of a reinvestment account needs to be made before the tax assessment of the first financial year becomes final and also applies to future years.

The balance of the profits and losses on securities (including unrealized ones) and on the sale of other investments can be added to the reinvestment account. If a fiscal investment institution has opted for a reinvestment account, the management costs are not fully deductible from the business income of the UCITS. In that case, only a proportional part of the management costs is deductible from the business income, whereas the other part reduces the reinvestment account. The management costs thus have to be spread among the income available for distribution and the reinvestment account.

The reinvestment account can be voluntarily decreased at any time, and must be decreased with an amount equal to the negative balance of gains and losses on the investments for the year. Apart from the limitation of the annual reservation, there is also an overall limitation. The account may never be higher than the lowest of (i) the fiscal equity (paid-up capital plus fiscal reserve plus the amount available for distribution) and (ii) the book value of the investments at the end of the year.

(b) *The round-off reserve*: In any tax year the fiscal investment institution can elect to add any amount to this reserve for the purpose of rounding-off profit distributions. The round-off reserve may, however, never exceed 1% of the paid-up capital. The reserve must be decreased when there is a fiscal loss and can be added to the fiscal profit if the company elects to do so.

4.10.3.5 Tax Treaty Eligibility

A fiscal investment institution is considered to be a resident for the purposes of the Netherlands tax treaties. It is liable to corporate income tax on its worldwide taxable income although at a tax rate of nil per cent. The latter should be viewed in combination with the requirement for fiscal investment institutions to distribute the income available for distribution to the shareholders annually, which guarantees the taxation of that income at the level of the shareholders. The application of tax treaties to a fiscal investment institution is, therefore, justified in the view of the Netherlands. This view is generally followed by the tax treaty partners.

4.10.3.6 Foreign Withholding Taxes

Under domestic law as well as under most tax treaties and the Tax Charter for the Kingdom of the Netherlands, the Netherlands has provided a credit for foreign withholding tax. In the case of fiscal investment institutions, no tax is due so a credit has no effect. For that reason, the Dividend Tax Act provides relief for source tax withheld on dividends and interest. The relief takes place in the form of a payment reduction for the tax that has to be withheld by the fiscal investment institution at the time of distribution to its shareholders. Any foreign withholding tax on dividend and interest may be set-off by a fiscal investment institution against the 15% tax that is withheld at the time of distribution. Hence, a fiscal investment institution does not have to pay the full amount of the withholding tax to the tax authorities while the tax withheld is fully creditable by the shareholders. The relief for foreign withholding tax is limited to 15% of the gross amount of the dividend or interest received by the fiscal investment institution.

A fiscal investment institution receives only a partial relief for foreign withholding tax if some of the non-resident shareholders other than pension funds or charities residing in the EU are under the Tax Charter for the Kingdom of the Netherlands or a tax treaty entitled to a reduction of or an exemption from withholding tax at the time of distribution (disqualifying shareholders).

4.11 INSURANCE COMPANIES

Article 29 CITA 69 provides for a general possibility of issuing special rules for insurance companies by decree, in particular in respect of the calculation of the tax base and the allowable reserves. In 2001, a decree to be referred to as the Insurance Tax base and Equalization Decree was issued. Through this decree a number of rules with respect to the annual calculation of the tax base of insurance companies is given (a dominant issue with insurance companies in this respect is at what time they have to report profits on the insurance policies they have issued). The decree also offers insurance companies the possibility of creating a tax-exempt equalization reserve. The Decree contains rules regarding contributions to the equalization reserve, as well as if and how the reserve must be decreased and partly or totally added to the fiscal result. In addition to this reserve the decree gives insurance companies the possibility of establishing a calamity reserve. This reserve is meant to cover nuclear risks.

4.12 NON-RESIDENT CORPORATIONS

4.12.1 Tax Base

A non-resident corporation is taxable only on its 'Netherlands taxable amount, which is defined as the annual Netherlands income minus the Netherlands losses of other years that can be set-off'. Article 17 CITA 69, which specifically applies to non-resident companies, describes the following sources of income:

(a) income from an enterprise carried on in the Netherlands by way of a permanent establishment or a permanent representative; and

(b) net income from a substantial interest in a company situated in the Netherlands provided the substantial interest is not a part of the enterprise carried out by the company holding the substantial interest (only substantial interests that are held as portfolio investment are taxed in the Netherlands).

In Article 17a CITA 69 the following items of income are also considered to be from Netherlands sources:

(a) Immovable property situated in the Netherlands, including:
  (i) rights directly or indirectly related to immovable property situated in the Netherlands; and
  (ii) rights associated with the exploration for and exploitation of natural resources present in the Netherlands including the production of energy from water, currents and winds, or rights to which they are subjected.
(b) Profit entitlements in a company situated in the Netherlands that have not accrued out of shares.
(c) Claims on a company established in the Netherlands in which the non-resident company has a substantial interest as referred to above (Article 17, paragraph 3, subparagraph (b) CITA 69).
(d) Activities as a director or a commissioner.
(e) Activities in, above or under the North Sea extraction site.

4.13 THE CORPORATE INCOME TAX RATE

The tax rate amounts to 20% of the first EUR 200,000 of the taxable amount and 25% of the excess over this amount.

Chapter 5
Wage Tax

5.1 GENERAL

Wage tax is levied on the basis of the Wage Tax Act 1965. It is a so-called direct tax which is levied from employees, artists, professional sportsmen and some other groups or persons mentioned in the law. In principle, wage tax is a kind of income tax levied through a withholding from the salary. It can either qualify as a prepaid tax which can be credited against the ultimate income tax, or as a final tax if no income tax is due. If the wage tax exceeds the income tax which is ultimately due, the difference will generally be refunded.

5.2 EMPLOYEE, EMPLOYMENT, WITHHOLDING AGENT

5.2.1 Employee

The tax is levied from the employee. An employee is defined as any individual who:

- is employed by a wage tax withholding agent; or
- receives wages from a wage tax withholding agent in connection with a former employment of himself or herself (e.g., a pension) or another person (i.e. a surviving relatives' pension); or
- receives wages of a withholding agent in connection with an employment of another person (e.g., study allowance paid by the employer of the father) on a voluntary basis.

5.2.2 Employment

The basis for the fiscal employment concept is the employment agreement as defined under civil law. This is an agreement whereby one party binds himself or herself to the other party to perform duties during a certain period in return for a salary. Such an agreement needs not necessarily be written down in a contract but may also be agreed verbally. A basic element of the employment agreement is the existence of authority at the level of the employer. This authority must result from the employment agreement or from facts and circumstances in absence of an agreement. This implies that the employee who is performing his or her duties is obliged to follow the directions of the employer. This does not, however, necessarily imply that the employee may not, for instance, choose his or her own working hours. In that case an employment relationship may still exist.

5.2.3 Withholding Agent

The Wage Tax Act does not refer to the employer as the person obliged to withhold the wage tax, but uses the word *Inhoudingsplichtige* (wage tax withholding agent). The definition of the 'wage tax withholding agent' is much wider than that of 'employer'. Consequently, it may also include persons or legal entities which are not employers such as a pension fund or an insurance company. The same applies to those institutions which administer and pay social security payments.

5.2.4 Deemed Employments

The Wage Tax Act also provides for deemed employments; that is, a labour relationship which would not qualify as an employment but which is deemed to be an employment for wage tax purposes. For example, the following persons may be considered to have a deemed employment:

- construction workers;
- persons who fall under the notional employment for wage tax (*gelijkgestelden*);
- home workers;
- director and major shareholder;
- members of the supervisory board (*commissarissen*).

5.3 THE TAX BASE

5.3.1 General Remarks

The tax base is the gross amount of wages. 'Wages' also includes rights to future income or distributions provided they are not based on payments by the employees. Through this system the claim on such income is taxed at the moment it arises. The future payments are in principle exempt. The right is valued at the amount paid by the employer. There are some exceptions to the rule that these rights are taxed if and when they arise. The most important example is the pension right. Rights to pension which qualify as pensions under the definition provided for in the Wage Tax Act are not taxed at the time the right is granted but at the time the pension is paid. Wages can also be paid in kind, such as goods, free housing, etc. There are a large number of detailed valuation tables to establish the value to be taken into account for tax purposes. As from 2011 there are introduced new regulations regarding the compensation of expenses and the provision in kind to avoid expenses for the wage tax (*werkkostenregeling*).

5.3.2 Stock Options

The benefit received by an employee via the granting of a stock option right by his or her employer is taxable income for the employee. Not the value of the right but the money the employee receives at the moment he or she cashes it, is taxed. The amount the employee had to pay for the option must then be deducted.

Special rules apply for the (non) taxation of the options if there has been a merger or a takeover of more than 50% of the shares of the employer or an affiliated company.

5.3.3 Employee Savings Plans

An employee savings plan is a plan, other than a pension plan, which allows an employee to set aside an amount of his or her wages to a special savings account. The contributions to an employee savings plan are taxed at a fixed rate of 25%. The contributions may, however, not be withdrawn for a period of four years, unless the money will be used for the acquisition of an owner-occupied dwelling, shares or some special premiums.

5.3.4 Free Remunerations

The wage tax contains some free remunerations as well as free benefits in kind. These are remunerations of costs made to fulfil an employment adequately, or for example free food eaten during working hours or for representation. Free benefits in kind can be transport of the employee from home to the place of work vice versa or free parking space at the place of work.

5.4 NON-RESIDENT EMPLOYEES

A non-resident employee will only be considered as an employee for wage tax purposes:

- if he or she is employed partly in the Netherlands; that is, performs his or her employment duties within the Netherlands;
- if he or she receives wages from a former employment carried on in the Netherlands; or
- if he or she is entitled to receive a benefit or certain facilities; for example, if he or she is entitled to a pension.

It is to be noted that a non-resident employer is only considered a wage tax withholding agent if he or she maintains a permanent establishment in the Netherlands, or if the tax inspector has appointed the non-resident employer as a wage tax withholding agent.

One condition to be met by the non-resident in order to be appointed as withholding agent is that the wage tax administration must be kept at an address in the Netherlands.

5.5 RATES

Given the relation between wage tax and income tax it is obvious that there is a relation between the rates used for wage tax purposes and the income tax rates. Basically, the tax rates are the same. There are some differences due to the difference in nature of both taxes. For wage tax purposes the regular wages will be taxed per period in which the wages are paid (week, month), but on the basis of a tax table which assumes that this amount will be paid during the whole year. Non-periodic wages are taxed at a special rate, which depends on the total wages. The wage tax tables are not included in this book.

5.6 PAYMENT OF THE TAX

Wage tax is levied by the self-assessment system (see section 2.4). It must be withheld from the wages and paid either monthly, quarterly or sometimes annually to the tax collector.

A special rule applies if the employer and the employee have agreed that the wages will not be paid in money (but in holiday vouchers for example) and be deferred to a later, irregular date. In such a case, the agreement has to be ignored for application of the wage tax and the employer has to withhold the wage tax relating to the deferred wages as if the deferral had not taken place.

5.7 LIABILITY IN CASE OF HIRING OF PERSONNEL

In the case of hiring of personnel, the company can be held liable for the wage tax if the person who hired out the personnel failed to withhold and pay wage tax and/or failed to pay VAT due according to the hiring contract.

5.8 LIABILITY IN CASE OF SUBCONTRACTING

Contractors can be held liable for the failure of sub-contractors to pay wage tax. Exceptions with respect to liability are:

- the subcontractor cannot be blamed for the non-payment of wage tax;
- the subcontractor performs all or most of his or her work at the place where his or her business is established;
- the work the subcontractor performs for the contractor is incidental to a contract for purchase and sale of an existing property.

The liability can sometimes be mitigated if special so-called blocked accounts (*G-rekeningen*) are used into which a part of the contract sum is paid.

5.9 WAGE TAX REDUCTION FOR RESEARCH AND DEVELOPMENT WORK

5.9.1 General

There is a bill regarding the facilitation of research and development work (hereafter R&D). Those entitled to the facility include entrepreneurs who are considered withholding agents for wage tax purposes and who perform R&D activities. A condition is that the withholding agent carry on an enterprise in the sense of ITA 1964 or CITA 69, or carry out R&D, an alliance of enterprises or a commodity board or industrial board (contract research). If the withholding agent is part of a fiscal unity in the sense of the CITA 69 and provides employees for R&D to an enterprise within this fiscal unity, upon request and under further conditions, the withholding agent will be deemed to perform the R&D himself or herself. Without such a request there would be no entitlement to the facility, either for the borrowing or for the lending company.

5.9.2 The Facility

The legislation provides for a reduction of wage tax and national insurance premiums payable by withholding agents (employers). The size of the reduction is related to the wage costs of the employees who carry out R&D.

5.9.3 Definition of R&D

According to the text of the bill, the term R&D is understood to be applicable to different groups and only for special costs.

These groups, each with his or her own set of rules, are:

(1) Education (see section 5.9.5)
(2) Research and Development Work (see section 5.9.6)
(3) Shipping (see section 5.9.7).

The bill has its own definition of employees and was enacted to stimulate employment and to promote education and research.

5.9.4 Obtaining the Facility

The withholding agent may, without approval of the tax inspector in advance, deduct the R&D facility from the wage tax payable. The wage tax payable, however, cannot become negative. In some cases the period for applying the reduction is a year, in some other cases the period is shorter. It varies per category and also depends of the number of hours worked.

5.9.5 Education

In some cases the bill also applies to wages paid during a period of study and education. For example, for employees who have an apprenticeship or a doctoral candidate at a University or training on the job.

5.9.6 Research and Development Work

This category needs a special declaration before the bill can be applied. The bill also applies to research and development work done outside the Netherlands but inside Europe.

5.9.7 Shipping

This category applies to wages paid to seafarers on board of a ship that has its port of registry in the Netherlands and performs special tasks like towing or dredging.

5.10 COMPULSORY IDENTIFICATION OF EMPLOYEES

On 1 June 1994 the Act on compulsory identification entered into force. This Act requires that in certain situations individuals should be able to prove their identity.

This Act also has far-reaching consequences for employers, since it compels employers to establish their employees' identity on the basis of a Dutch passport, a European identity card or a foreign passport, if necessary together with a residence permit.

The obligation refers to employees who receive wages from current employment, and not to pensioners. The employer is not allowed to establish his or her employees' identity on the basis of, for instance, a driving license. The employer is obliged to record the type, number and a photocopy of the identification document with the wage records. If requested, the inspector may also allow the information to be stored elsewhere; for instance, at the place where the activities are actually carried on. Instead of making a photocopy, the employer may also include the document in a computer file by means of a scanner.

There is a heavy sanction for the employer on not complying with this obligation: a fine of EUR 4,920 (2011).

5.11 THE 30% RULING

5.11.1 General

Since 1970 a special concession has been available to foreign employees (expatriates) assigned to the Netherlands. If certain requirements were met, the employee was eligible for a special 35% deduction from his or her employment income. The claim in income tax return was 35%, has been changed and it is now 30% and is given in the wage tax.

The former 35% ruling was in principle only granted to employees who were assigned, within an international group, to a Dutch group company or branch office located in the Netherlands. The new 30% ruling may also be granted to employees who are not transferred within an international group.

5.11.2 Conditions of the New 30% Ruling

The facility applies to employees who have been recruited by a Dutch employer and who fulfils certain conditions and also for Dutch employees assigned abroad.

In order to qualify for the 30% ruling, the foreign employee has to be posted from another country to a domestic employer (i.e. a party which is obliged to withhold Dutch wage tax) or recruited from abroad by a domestic employer, provided:

- the employee lives or stays and actually carries out his or her employment in the Netherlands;
- the employee is in the employ of a wage tax withholding agent;
- the domestic employer makes it plausible that he or she has employed the foreign employee or that the employee has been posted to him or her

because the employee has specific expertise which is not available or scarce in the Dutch employment market, so that this employee could only be recruited abroad.

So under the new ruling, the following factors, viewed in their mutual context, play a role in assessing the specific expertise:

- the required experience and/or expertise or education/training was acquired outside the Netherlands and is not available or is scarce in the Netherlands;
- the function of the foreign employee requires specific qualifications;

According to the tax authorities, a work-permit (which must be obtained by a non-EU national) will give a strong indication that the foreign employee has specific expertise which is not available or scarce on the Dutch labour market.

5.11.3 Duration of the Ruling

The new 30% ruling is available for a maximum period of 10 years starting from the commencement of the employment in the Netherlands.

The above-mentioned period is reduced by the duration of any earlier stay or earlier periods of employment in the Netherlands. However, if the actual date of the foreign employee's departure from the Netherlands was 15 years before the commencement of the employment for which a request to apply the 30% ruling was submitted, then the earlier stay or periods of employment will not be taken into account.

5.11.4 Application for the Ruling

Employees who are sent to the Netherlands need an official decision for the application of the 30% rule. In order to apply for the ruling a request must be made to the Tax Department for Non-resident Individuals and Foreign Companies in Brunssum. The request must be made jointly by or on behalf of the foreign employee and the domestic employer. For expatriate employees no decision is needed.

According to the new ruling, the foreign employer allows to grant a tax-free lump sum allowance for the extra costs of the employee's stay in the Netherlands (extraterritorial costs). The school fees for international schools for the children of the employees may also reimbursed free of tax. This remuneration can amount to 30% of the so-called calculation basis. This basis consists of the taxable wage as defined in the Wage Tax Act 1964 which is received in respect of the employment performed in the Netherlands and for which the foreign employee is subject to tax, plus the tax-free part. The 30% rule means that you can, without further proof, provide a free allowance of 30% including the reimbursement of pay, or 30/70 of the gross wage compensation as a free allowance for extraterritorial expenses. The maximum tax-free remuneration is 30% of the resulting amount.

The split of remuneration of the employee (in salary and cost allowance) should be effectuated in the payroll administration as soon as possible. In a formula it is 30% of 100/70 × gross wage.

These costs can include amongst others:

- additional costs of living due to higher prices (cost of living allowance);
- costs of travelling to the country of origin for family matters;
- cost of double housing;
- compensation for higher tax rates in the country of work.

Chapter 6

Social Security System

6.1 GENERAL

The Netherlands has the disposal of a very extensive social security system, comprising:

- *National Insurance Schemes:*
  - general old age pensions act (AOW);
  - general widows' and orphans' benefits act (ANW);
  - exceptional medical expenses act (AWBZ);
- *Employed Persons Insurance Schemes:*
  - sickness benefits act (ZW);
  - disablement insurance act (WIA);
  - healthcare insurance act (ZVW);
  - unemployment insurance act (WW).

6.2 NATIONAL INSURANCE SCHEMES

6.2.1 General

Insured under the national insurance schemes are all residents and most employees who are subject to the wages withholding tax.

6.2.2 Premium

The premium due for the national insurance schemes amounts to 31.15% over the first EUR 33,436 of taxable income. (In 2011, the percentage for AOW is 17.9%, for ANW 1.10% and AWBZ 12.15%.)

The premiums are due from the employee.

6.2.3 Procedures

The premiums are levied via withholding and via assessments. The employer withholds the premium from the wages. The premium withheld will be credited against the premium due on assessment. The income tax return serves as the return for the national insurance. The premiums due are included in the income tax assessment.

The premium is not tax deductible.

6.3 EMPLOYED PERSONS INSURANCE SCHEMES

6.3.1 General

Insured under the employed persons insurance schemes are employees who live in the Netherlands and have a resident employer or employees who perform their activities within the Netherlands. Also insured for employed persons insurance schemes are non-residents who have a resident employer and who perform their activities (partly) within the Netherlands.

6.3.2 Procedures

The employed persons insurance premiums are due from both the employer and the employee. The employee premiums are levied via withholding.

The premiums due from the employees, apart from the premium for the ZVW, are tax deductible.

6.3.3 Liability in Case of Hiring of Personnel

In the case of hiring of personnel, the company can be held liable for the national insurance premiums and employed persons insurance premiums if the person who hired out the personnel failed to withhold and pay wage tax and/or failed to pay the VAT due on respect to the hiring contract. The liability can be mitigated if special so-called blocked accounts are used into which a part of the contract sum is paid.

6.3.4 Liability in Case of Subcontracting

Contractors can be held liable for the national insurance premiums and employed persons insurance premiums due from sub-contractors. Exceptions with respect to liability are:

(1) the contractor nor the subcontractor can be blamed for the non-payment of the premiums;
(2) the subcontractor performs all or most of his or her work at the place where his or her business is established;
(3) the work the subcontractor performs for the contractor is incidental to a contract for purchase and sale of existing property; or
(4) the contractor has paid a sum corresponding to the amount of premiums due, unto a blocked account, specifically opened for this purpose. Any payment from such an account can only be made to the tax receiver or another similar blocked account.

The liability can be mitigated if special so-called blocked accounts are used into which a part of the contract sum is paid.

Chapter 7
Dividend Withholding Tax

7.1 INTRODUCTION

The Netherlands levies a withholding tax on dividends (hereafter referred to as withholding tax). No withholding tax is levied on interest or royalties, although these items may sometimes be subject to income tax. The tax is withheld on the basis of the (Dividend) Withholding Tax Act of 1965 (DWTA 65). Like the wages tax, the withholding tax has a dual character. If the income is subject to withholding it is liable either to income tax or corporate income tax. The withholding tax can be credited against these taxes as a prepaid tax. In those cases where the income subject to withholding is neither subject to income tax nor to corporate income tax, the withholding represents the final (Netherlands) tax on that income.

7.2 TAXABLE PERSONS

According to Article 1 DWTA 65 the withholding tax is levied from persons (individuals as well as legal entities) who are entitled to the proceeds from:

- shares;
- profit-sharing certificates;
- hybrid loans;
- certificates;

that have been issued by:

- corporations (NVs or BVs);
- so-called open limited partnerships;
- any other corporation with a capital divided into shares (other kind of stock corporations).

Provided these entities are resident of the Netherlands for tax purposes.

Investment participations issued by investment associations are treated equally as shares in a joint stock corporation.

Dividend paid by exempt investment institutions as meant in Article 6a CITA 69 are not subject to dividend withholding tax.

The third paragraph of Article 1 DWTA 65 also provides that, for the application of the withholding tax, a corporation or other legal entity is deemed to be a resident of the Netherlands if it is incorporated under Netherlands law (a similar provision has been made in the CITA). A so-called European corporation that is a corporation ruled by Netherlands law, also falls under this article.

However, it should be noted that this provision can be set aside as a result of a tax treaty. For example, in 1992, the Dutch Supreme Court rendered a decision in the following case. Since its formation, the place of effective management of a Dutch BV was situated in Ireland. The company carried on an enterprise in Ireland and did not derive income from Dutch sources. Its shares were held by a US company. The Irish BV distributed a dividend to its parent company. According to the Supreme Court, no Dutch dividend withholding tax was due. The Supreme Court based its decision on Article 8, paragraph 9 of the Dutch-Irish treaty, which is similar to Article 10, paragraph 5 of the OECD-Model Double Taxation Convention. This provision rules out extraterritorial taxation of dividends. According to the Supreme Court, the principle of non-extraterritorial taxation also applies if the dividends are distributed to a person who is a resident of a State other than the contracting States.

7.3 THE TAX BASE

7.3.1 General

Tax is withheld from any proceeds derived from the shares, certificates, etc., mentioned in section 8.2. The following proceeds are specifically included:

(a) distributions of profit (either directly or indirectly), official or disguised (like redemption of shares) under whatever name or in whatever form;
(b) liquidation proceeds to the extent they exceed the average paid-up capital;
(c) stock dividends – not being stock dividends out of the share premiums reserve (agio) – for their nominal value, less the amount of capital to be paid up by the shareholder;
(d) repayment of paid-in capital to the extent the net asset value (including hidden reserves) exceeds the amount of the paid-in capital, unless the paid-in capital has been reduced accordingly through an official change (by the general meeting of shareholders) of the articles of association;
(e) payments on profit-sharing certificates, as well as all payments in respect of repurchase or redemption thereof;
(f) reimbursement for hybrid loans;

(g) repayment of paid-in capital to the extend that the net asset value of the fund exceeds the amount of the paid in-capital;
(h) under certain conditions the payment on investments participations.

Payments in kind are valued at market value (exception, see point (c)).

7.3.2 Paid-In Capital

The concept of paid-in capital is very important as it can be repaid free of dividend withholding tax. As of 1989, the DWTA provides that in case of share-for-share transactions, the paid-in capital of a Netherlands company is only increased by the original paid-in capital of the transferred company, and not the fair market value of the transferred shares at the moment of the transaction. According to this rule, a Netherlands dividend withholding tax claim would be created on profits from abroad obtained during a period before the shares in a foreign company were transferred to a Netherlands company.

Therefore, the fair market value of the transferred stock of the foreign subsidiary can be recognized for tax purposes as paid-in capital of the Netherlands company in case of a share-for-share transfer, provided certain conditions are met.

However, in case of dividend distributions, a so-called last-in first-out system will apply, which means that profits obtained after the shares of the foreign corporation were transferred, are supposed to be distributed first. Interested parties can contact the tax inspector and give notice of distributions which have their origin in foreign profits obtained before the exchange of shares. If the tax inspector considers it plausible that the distributions do not originate from profits obtained after the exchange of shares, no dividend tax will be due.

7.4 EXEMPTIONS

No tax is withheld for example:

(a) if the shares in the hands of the recipient are a participation as meant in Article 13/13aa CITA 69, provided the shares belong to the domestic assets of the recipient;
(b) if the profits are distributed to a parent company resident in the EU, provided a number of requirements are met;
(c) if the recipient company and the distributing company are part of the same fiscal unity as meant in Article 15 CITA 69, provided the shares belong to the domestic assets of the recipient;
(d) if the profits are distributed to a parent company resident in the EU/Iceland/Norway and the shares in the hands of the recipient are a participation as meant in Article 13/13aa CITA 69, provided a number of requirements are met;
(e) redemption of shares of listed corporations and authorized investment funds, provided certain conditions are met.

7.5 THE TAX RATE

The rate amounts to 15%. The only exceptions are the so-called recapitalization dividend and income from shares derived within two years after the shares were acquired through inheritance by the taxpayer, up to one-third of the value of the shares thus acquired.

Where the withholding tax is borne by the paying entity the tax is grossed up by 100/85.

7.6 THE WAY IN WHICH THE TAX IS LEVIED

The withholding tax is levied through a compulsory withholding by the company or other entity distributing the income at the time it is made available. That entity pays the tax to the tax collector (self-assessment).

It may be set-off against the income tax and works just like the wage tax like an advance levy (see Article 9.2 ITA 2001 and Article 25, paragraph 2 CITA 69).

The company is also obliged to issue an official notice of dividend payment (tax voucher), indicating, among other things, the amount of the dividend as well as the tax withheld. This document can be used by the recipient to reclaim or credit the withholding tax.

Foreign dividend withholding tax, under specific circumstances, can be credited against the Dutch dividend withholding tax due, see Article 11 DWTA 65. The credit applies if foreign dividends, qualifying for the participation exemption, are redistributed by a Dutch company. The tax credit is limited to 3%. The distributing company will still have to withhold dividend withholding tax at the standard rate from the dividend distribution. However, as a result of the credit the Dutch company has to pay less tax to the tax collector.

7.7 REFUND OF WITHHOLDING TAX

Certain resident and EU/Icelandic/Norwegian corporations or legal entities not subject to corporate income tax may request a refund of withholding tax provided they owned the security on which the dividend was paid for a period exceeding three months. Article 11a DWTA 65 gives some more specific rules for investment institutions.

7.8 FILING OF RETURN

The withholding tax is levied on the basis of the self-assessment system. The return must be filed and paid within one month after the dividend has been declared.

Chapter 8
Value Added Tax (BTW)

8.1 GENERAL

On 1 January 1969, a turnover tax based on a VAT system was introduced in the Netherlands on the basis of the second EC Directive concerning the harmonization of turnover tax systems. The official Dutch name of this turnover tax is *Omzetbelasting* (abbreviated OB), but another name often used is *Belasting over de toegevoegde waarde*, in short: BTW.

As of 1 January 1979 the Netherlands legislation has been adapted to the provisions of the sixth EC Directive, which provides for a far-reaching unification of the various European value added tax Acts. Since 1 January 1993 the fiscal frontiers within the EU have been abolished. However, the 27 Member States have not formed one territory for tax purposes. Only the fiscal border controls have disappeared. The unification process still continues. On 1 January 2007, all VAT-directives (including the sixth EC Directive) have been replaced by the VAT-Directive.

The turnover tax on a value added basis, as in force in the Netherlands, is levied at the various economic trading levels down to and including the retail trade. VAT does not, however, have a cumulative effect because of the deduction of tax paid in previous stages. Every taxpayer is liable to VAT on his or her turnover but may compensate such tax with the VAT which has been charged to him or her on expenses and investments.

A positive balance must be paid to the tax collector. A negative balance will be reimbursed by the tax collector. The ultimate result will be a tax burden equal to the applicable VAT percentage on the consumer price; that is, the price paid by a person who is not entitled to a deduction of prepaid VAT (see Table 8.1).

Table 8.1. Example – VAT Percentage 19%

			Payment to the Tax Authorities
Supplier of Raw Materials	Sale	100 + 19.0 VAT	19.0
Manufacturer	Sale	200 + 38.0 VAT	
	Purchase	100 + 19.0 VAT	19.0
Wholesale Dealer	Sale	260 + 49.4 VAT	
	Purchase	200 + 38.0 VAT	11.4
Retailer	Sale	360 + 68.4 VAT	
	Purchase	260 + 49.4 VAT	19.0
Total			68.4

The ultimate buyer, the consumer, suffers a total VAT-burden of 19% on 360 or 68.4 which is the aggregate of the VAT levied through the different economic transition levels.

Because of the possibility of direct deduction the VAT is usually not a financial burden for the entrepreneur. If the deliveries or the services of the entrepreneur are (partly) exempt, the entrepreneur will not become (full) deduction, in that case it can (partly) become a financial burden (see Table 8.2).

Table 8.2. Example per Tax Payer – Garage

		VAT 19%
Turnover in January:		
car sales	4,000,000	760,000
repairs	100,000	19,000
fuel	80,000	15,200
	4,180,000	794,200
Purchases January:		
Cars	3,000,000	570,000
Materials	20,000	3,800
Fuel	60,000	11,400
Investments: garage building	2,000,000	380,000
	5,080,000	965,200
VAT due		794,200
to be refunded		171,000

The effect of the VAT system is that the burden is equal to the VAT percentage on the consumer price regardless of the number of total transactions (internal neutrality).

As Dutch VAT is supposed to tax only the consumption of goods and services within the Netherlands, their export to other EU countries as well as to third countries is effectively freed from tax by taxing the exporter under the so-called zero-rate. This has the effect that no tax is due whereas the prepaid tax can nevertheless be deducted or may be reimbursed. Imported goods are subject to the same VAT-burden as domestic goods (external neutrality).

8.2 THE TAXPAYER

The taxable person is the person liable for VAT. This often is an entrepreneur (in VAT language), but due to some special regulations, can also be an individual. In general, VAT is levied from entrepreneurs in respect of deliveries of goods and/or the performance of services, carried out within the scope of an enterprise (Article 1, Value Added Tax Act 1968, hereafter referred to as VATA 68).

An entrepreneur is anyone who carries on a business independently (Article 7 VATA 68). An enterprise is defined as an organization of capital and labour with the permanent aim of satisfying needs by participation in the economic process. The legal structure of the enterprise is irrelevant for VAT purposes.

Legal entities (NV, BV, foundation, etc.), individuals (in private enterprises or professions) and also combinations of them and associations (partnerships) can be considered entrepreneurs if they carry on a business. It is not necessary to carry on business with a view to a profit.

In principle, neither nationality nor residence are relevant. A foreign entrepreneur who carries on taxable activities in the Netherlands is also subject to VAT, although the way in which the VAT is actually levied may differ.

Combinations of enterprises which form a unity from a financial, organizational, and economic viewpoint can be deemed to constitute a fiscal unity for VAT purposes. Where a unity is recognized, deliveries and services within it are not subject to VAT.

Public entities (the State, provinces or municipalities, etc.) are in principle also liable to VAT on their deliveries of goods and supply of services, unless they act within the scope of their public duties; that is, to accomplish tasks within a special (public) regime. All other transactions (such as real estate transactions) by these public entities are in principle liable to VAT in any case.

VAT on importation of goods and on intra-Community acquisition of goods (especially of new means of transportation) will also be levied of private persons.

8.3 THE TAXABLE OBJECT

There are four taxable events (Article 1 VATA 68):

(a) Supplies of goods and services within the Netherlands by entrepreneurs.
(b) Intra-Community acquisitions of goods in the Netherlands by entrepreneurs and corporations, other than entrepreneurs.

(c) Intra-Community acquisitions of new means of transportation in the Netherlands, regardless by whom.
(d) Importation of goods regardless by whom.

8.3.1 Supply of Goods

In the first place VATA 68 refers to civil law by considering any contractual transfer of ownership as a delivery for VAT purposes.

In addition, the following acts are considered as 'deliveries for VAT purposes' by entrepreneurs:

- the transfer of goods on the basis of a hire-purchase agreement;
- a delivery of goods by a manufacturer who has manufactured the goods from materials supplied by the customer;
- the transfer of goods as a result of which the goods effectively leave the beneficial ownership of an enterprise (e.g., an economic transfer of ownership);
- the private use of goods by an entrepreneur;
- the self-manufactured goods which are used for exempt transactions for which prepaid tax cannot be deducted or is only partly deductible;
- the transfer of goods by a taxable person from his or her enterprise to another Member State;
- the legal transfer of goods on payment of a redress in consequence of a collection by or on behalf of public authorities/government;
- the legal transfer of goods that are subject to an agreement to affix those goods to other goods;
- the establishment of property rights, with the exception of mortgage and ground rent, unless the redress contains less than the market value price of the property rights.

8.3.2 Supply of Services

Services are defined as all performances for a consideration not qualifying as a delivery of goods as referred to above (Article 4 VATA 68). A service for which no consideration is received is not taxable. The service concept is very broadly defined. Apart from carrying out certain activities for a consideration, it also includes an agreement that certain activities should not be performed. The transfer of rights and the abandoning of rights for a consideration are also considered services.

If goods forming part of the assets of a business and are used for private purposes and if services are used for private purposes for which no consideration is received, this is also considered to be a service.

8.3.3 Intra-community Acquisitions

The intra-Community acquisition of goods is defined as the acquisition of the right to dispose as owner of movable tangible property dispatched or transported to a Member State other than that from which the goods are dispatched or transported, pursuant to a supply by another entrepreneur.

As regards transactions between taxable persons within different EU Member States, supplies of goods are taxed at 0% VAT in the Member State of which the supplier is a resident. The supplier retains the right to deduct input tax. The goods are taxed in the Member State where the goods arrive. The tax must be declared by the purchaser. If he or she has a right to deduct input VAT, the amount of VAT due is deductible.

Some non-entrepreneurs are treated as entrepreneurs for acquisition purposes. Farmers under the flat-rate scheme, entrepreneurs that only perform exempt transactions and legal entities other than entrepreneurs, perform taxable intra-Community acquisitions if their purchases exceed EUR 10,000 or have exceeded EUR 10,000 in the past year.

Special rules apply to the administration of intra-Community transactions.

8.3.4 Intra-community Acquisitions of New Means of Transport

An intra-Community acquisition can also be performed by individuals (non-entrepreneurs) when purchasing new means of transport from another Member State. A means of transport is new when it has been used for less than six months if it is a car and in case it is a ship or aircraft the time-limit is three months, or, if it is a:

- car (minimum 48 cc) if it has been driven less than 6,000 km;
- ship (minimum length 7.5 m) if it has been sailed less than 100 hours;
- aircraft (minimum weight 1,550 kg) if it has been flown less than 40 hours.

The consequence of such a purchase is that the individual has to pay VAT in the Member State where the goods are delivered.

8.3.5 Importation of Goods

The importation of goods from non-EU countries is taxable regardless of whether the importer is an entrepreneur. The VAT on importation is due on the basis of bringing the goods into the country and is levied according to the rules of the import duty legislation (Article 18 VATA 68). A number of exemptions applying to import duties also apply to VAT, such as the exemptions for: diplomatic goods; importation of furniture belonging to a household upon transfer of residence; re-importation of goods sent abroad for processing or repairing.

8.3.6 Place of Deliveries and Services

Only the supply of goods and services as well as the intra-Community acquisition of goods within the Netherlands is subject to Dutch value added tax. For this reason it is always essential to establish the place where the taxable transaction is performed. This is not always the actual place of supply, since special rules exist under VAT law deeming some supplies and services to take place elsewhere.

8.3.6.1 Place of Supply of Goods (Article 5 and 5a VATA 68)

(a) For goods which are transported for supply, the place of delivery is deemed to be the place where the transportation started, unless there is talk of the transfer of goods which are subject to an agreement to assemble those goods to other goods.
(b) In other cases the supply is deemed to take place where goods are located at the time of delivery.
(c) A supply of goods on board of a ship, aircraft or train and during a passenger transport with departure and arrival in the EU, is deemed to take place at the point of departure.
(d) In case of a chain of subsequent transactions of goods to be imported from outside the EU, the place of all supplies is deemed to be in the Member State of import. A zero-rate is charged in respect of all the transactions before supply to the actual importer insofar as the goods are imported by or on behalf of the supplier.
(e) If a supply of goods, other than new means of transport, is transported to a recipient in the Netherlands from another Member State for the account of the supplier, the delivery is deemed to take place in the Netherlands, if:
   - the total amount of goods sent by the supplier to the Netherlands is more than EUR 100,000 or was more than EUR 100,000 in the preceding calendar year and;
   - the recipient is an individual; or
   - the recipient is a farmer under the flat-rate scheme, an entrepreneur that only performs exempt transactions, or a legal entity other than entrepreneur, if their purchases amount to less than EUR 10,000 in the current and in the previous year.

Similar provisions apply in other Member States, although the threshold in some Member States may be lower than EUR 100,000.

Under certain conditions the entrepreneur can choose the place of delivery for the place of supply of goods.

Supplies of excise goods that are transported to a recipient in another Member State for the account of the supplier are deemed to be in the country where the goods are delivered.

Triangular transactions which involve parties each located in a different EU Member State, selling goods which are transported from one EU Member State to another, could cause complicated VAT positions.

The simplification rule on these transactions effectively allows the middleman to avoid registering for VAT in the country of dispatch or destination, provided he or she designates his or her buyer to pay for the VAT in the country of destination.

For the Netherlands, the simplification can be applied as follows.

The sale from the supplier of the goods, (A), to the middleman, (B), is taxable in the country of dispatch against the 0% rate, provided that B provides A with his or her VAT-identification number in his or her own (EU Member State) country. B may not be registered for VAT purposes in country A.

B reports an acquisition of the goods to his or her VAT authorities and accounts for VAT, which is also directly recoverable. Buyer C accounts for local VAT on the delivery from B by the way of a reversed charge procedure; that is, C is liable for this VAT, but will be able to offset this VAT as input VAT in most cases. B as well as C will have to report their transaction to their respective VAT authorities in order for them to 'match' the transactions.

This means that B will have to invoice to C, using C's VAT-identification number, and should refer to the simplified procedure with the statement.

The parties may waive this simplified procedure, but if they do, B will have to register in one of the two countries involved in the transportation of goods. The procedure is not applicable if B is not registered for VAT purposes in any EU Member State.

8.3.6.2 Place of Supply of Services (Article 6 and 6a VATA 68)

As of 1 January 2010, the general rule for place of supply of services has changed. For taxation of services from business to business the general rule is that that services are supplied where the consumer is established (or maintains a permanent establishment). In this connection a legal entity not being an entrepreneur will be judged as an entrepreneur on condition that this legal entity is identified for VAT-drawing. The concept of taxable person has changed. For taxation of services from business to consumer the general rule is that services are supplied where the supplier is established (or maintains a permanent establishment from which the services are supplied). There are several exceptions to these rules:

(a) Services by an intermediary, who acts in the name of and for account of a third party, delivered to a non-entrepreneur are deemed to be supplied where the act/work/deal has been accomplished.
(b) Services in respect of real estate are deemed to be supplied where the real estate is situated.
(c) The place of transportation of persons is the place where the transportation is effected. Thus, the transportation is deemed to be effected in the Netherlands to the extent the transportation takes place within the country.

(d) The place of transportation of goods for non-entrepreneurs is the place where transportation is effected, pro rata the travelled distances (however, see point (e) for an important exception to this rule).
(e) For intra-Community transport of goods for non-entrepreneurs, the main rule is that services are deemed to be rendered at the place of delivery.
(f) Services related to intra-Community transport, such as loading and unloading, for others than entrepreneurs are deemed to be rendered at the location where the activities actually take place. For investigations and activities related to tangible goods the same rule is effected.
(g) The place of services related to cultural, artistic, sportive, scientific, educative, amusement activities or similar activities are deemed to be supplied where the activities take place.
(h) The place of restaurant and catering services is where the services take place.
(i) Short-term car rental (with a maximum of 30 days) is deemed to be supplied at the place the car actually is placed at the disposal of the renter. The same rule applies to ships if the short-term rental is maximum 90 days.
(j) Electronic services rendered to a non-entrepreneurs in a Member State, by non-EU entrepreneurs are taxable where the purchasers have a permanent residence.
(k) Services for others than entrepreneurs, who have their residence outside the EU, have their own special rules. If the service concerns, among others, copyrights and advertising, advice, information, banking and insurance services, its place is generally considered to be rendered where the purchaser has his or her residence.
(l) If the service provider of a business to business supply is not established (nor maintains a permanent establishment) in the Netherlands, and the recipient has a VAT-identification number in the Netherlands, the recipient will be taxed.

8.3.6.3 Place of Intra-Community Acquisitions

Intra-Community acquisition of goods are deemed to take place in the Member State where the goods arrive at the end of the intra-Community transport.

8.4 THE TAX BASIS

VAT is levied on the consideration, that is the total amount, except the VAT itself, which has been charged in connection with the taxable transaction. In case of remuneration in kind, the value thereof will be taxed. For some specific deliveries – the private use of goods, as well as the use of self-manufactured goods – the taxable basis is the purchase price or the manufacturing cost.

In the case of the establishment of certain property rights such as a long lease, the rent charge is capitalized based on special schedules.

The remuneration does not include:

(a) the VAT itself;
(b) rebate for cash payments provided the rebate is shown on the invoice;
(c) cost of return packing;
(d) insurance expenses paid to an insurance company;
(e) expenses paid in the name of and for the account of a third party;
(f) taxes paid in the entrepreneur's own name but for the account of a third party;
(g) additional financing charges for deliveries which are paid by instalments (finance lease etc.).

In the case of importation the basis is the importation value (which equals customs value according to EU and General Agreement on Tariffs and Trade (GATT) rules).

8.5 TAX RATES AND EXEMPTIONS

The general rate presently amounts to 19%. There are two exceptions.

(a) The lower rate which presently amounts to 6% for various specifically mentioned goods and services (schedule I) such as:
  - various foodstuffs;
  - cattle, sheep, goats, pigs, horses, hatching eggs, poultry;
  - art, antiques, gold, silver, etc.;
  - books;
  - medicines, dressing materials, artificial limbs;
  - water;
  - certain goods and services for agricultural use;
  - repair of bicycles, footwear, clothing, kitchen linen;
  - transportation of persons;
  - admittance to circuses, zoos, museums, cinemas, sporting events, attraction parks;
  - the provision of rooms and meals by hotels and restaurants.

(b) The so-called zero-rate applies, amongst other things, to:
  - export of goods and the supply of goods to a bonded warehouse;
  - supply of goods that have not been imported, to the importer, and to deliveries prior to that;
  - sea-going vessels and aircrafts, used for international public means of transport;
  - gold for central banks;
  - services directly linked to import and export of goods such as loading, unloading and transportation;
  - services by agents for deliveries and supplying of services rendered outside the Netherlands;
  - intra-Community supplies of goods.

Apart from the lower rates, some supplies are exempted. These exemptions are:

- the transfer or rental of real estate (with certain exceptions);
- medical services;
- various social and cultural services;
- most services performed by banks;
- insurance transactions;
- postal, telephone and telegraph services;
- the supply of movable goods which have been exclusively used for exempt purposes.

8.6 DEDUCTIONS

In general, the prepaid tax which can be allocated to exempt supplies cannot be deducted (the prepaid tax attributable to zero-rated and low rated turnover is fully deductible). An exception to this rule is financial services to recipients outside the EU. For these services the prepaid tax can be deducted.

8.7 THE SETTING-OFF OF TAX

The VAT system implies that the entrepreneur may in principle deduct the VAT paid in respect of expenses or investments, from the VAT due on his or her turnover. A negative balance will be refunded by the VAT authorities. However, not all the prepaid tax may be deducted. A summary of the deductible and non-deductible prepaid tax (Article 15 of the VATA 68) is given below.

(a) Deductible prepaid VAT

VAT on expenses and investments which can be allocated to either taxable domestic turnover, or export transactions which are not at the same time exempt. A general condition is that the VAT has been charged on an invoice which satisfies the legal requirements (Article 35 of the VATA).

- The VAT due on the importation of goods.
- The VAT due on the intra-Community acquisition of goods.
- The VAT to be paid by the recipient of the goods or services on the basis of Article 12 VATA 68.
- The VAT due on the self-delivery of goods.
- The VAT to be paid as a result of using goods for business purposes.
- Under certain conditions the tax included in the purchase price of a new means of transport.

(b) Non-deductible prepaid VAT

- The VAT on expenses and investments which can be allocated to exempt transactions (transactions mentioned in Article 11 VATA 68). In case of use for both taxable and exempt transactions the prepaid tax must be split in the same ratio as the exempt/taxable turnover (pro rata

system) or on the basis of the actual use of the purchased goods and services.
- The VAT on restaurant expenditure for meals and drinks.
- The VAT on expenditure for gifts (including gifts to business acquaintances), wages in kind, provisions for staff.
- The VAT on tobacco products.
- The VAT on goods and services applied to keep up a certain position.
- The VAT on providing residence, remuneration in kind, sport application and entertainment for employees.

For movable assets and real estate the deduction is not exclusively based on the use in the year of acquisition but the deduction is readjusted on a pro rata time basis (positively as well as negatively) if the use and thus the deductibility have changed in the years subsequent to the year of acquisition (for movable assets up to four years and for real estate up to nine years). In this connection an exempt delivery within the reallocation period will fictionally be considered to be for an exempt use for the remaining part of the readjustment period. A taxable delivery within that period will be deemed a taxable use for that remaining period.

8.8 SPECIAL SUBJECTS

Several subjects deserve special attention because of special rules, for example:

- the delivery of real estate;
- rental of real estate;
- the integration levy (self-delivery);
- the regulations for small entrepreneurs;
- the regulations for farmers;
- the procedure for tax on imported goods and services;
- non-resident entrepreneurs;
- the shift of the tax liability (*verleggingsregeling*) on sub-contracting in the building industry and in the ready-made clothing industry.

8.8.1 The Delivery of Real Estate

The basic rule is that deliveries of real estate are exempt (Article 11, VATA 68). However, the following deliveries are taxable:

(a) constructed real estate until two years after the first use, and building land;
(b) real estate where supplier and recipient have applied for a taxable delivery.

The apply for a delivery subject to tax under (b) is related to the adjustment of prepaid tax as explained in section 8.7(b). In the case of an exempt delivery within the 10-year period there will be a fictitious exempt use and as a result the deducted prepaid tax must be revised and partly repaid. An apply for a taxable delivery will give rise to a fictitious taxable use so that no retroactive adjustment is necessary.

In case of exempt use – without a tax deduction – a taxable delivery within the 10-year period will give rise to a readjustment. In this case a pro rata refund of prepaid tax will be granted. The adjustment (Article 13a of the VAT Decree) will be made on a pro rata time basis. If a purchase is made subject to VAT the 10-year period will start again from that moment. The two-year period is applied once for all and will only be reapplied in the case of a new building activity (demolition, substantial alteration of the building, etc.).

8.8.2 Lease of Real Estate

Lease of real estate is exempt from VAT (Article 11, paragraph 1.b, VATA 68) with the exception of among others:

- the rental of permanent installed machinery;
- rental for use in a hotel and restaurant business;
- the rental of parking places for vehicles and the rental of accommodation and storage buildings for vessels;
- the rental of safe deposit boxes;
- rental of real estate (with the exception of private homes) whereby the lessor as well as the lessee have elected for rent subjected to VAT.

In particular, the apply for rental subjected to VAT is an important exception to the exemption, as this will enable the lessor to reclaim the VAT levied on investments and expenses attributable to the property.

Lessors who are portfolio investors rather than entrepreneurs can also elect for a rental to be subjected to VAT, as the exploitation of an asset in order to receive a long-term return is deemed to be an entrepreneurial activity.

8.8.3 Shift of the Tax at Importation

As mentioned in section 9.3.4, the importation of goods is subject to VAT. This VAT must in principle be paid at the time of the importation. Entrepreneurs who paid VAT on imported goods can treat this VAT as prepaid VAT in their periodic domestic VAT return. On the basis of Article 23 of the VATA 68 it is possible to synchronize the VAT due upon importation with the filing of the domestic VAT return in which the deduction is claimed.

VAT is then no longer paid at the border but reported as a liability in the return. The same amount is reported in the same return as prepaid VAT but only, of course, to the extent that a deduction as prepaid VAT is allowed on the basis of the general rules. This system among others applies to a specially designated group of goods (raw materials) and for other imports if the entrepreneur has officially requested and received permission.

The system does not extend to non-Dutch resident entrepreneurs who do not maintain a permanent establishment in the Netherlands.

8.8.4 The Non-resident Entrepreneur

A non-resident entrepreneur can be subject to tax if he or she performs taxable transactions in the Netherlands even if he or she does not maintain a permanent establishment in the Netherlands. A non-resident entrepreneur who maintains a permanent establishment in the Netherlands is treated as a domestic entrepreneur. Special provisions apply to a non-resident entrepreneur who does not maintain a permanent establishment in the Netherlands.

(a) Taxable transactions in the Netherlands

If a non-resident entrepreneur performs a taxable supply of goods or services to a domestic entrepreneur, to a foreign entrepreneur's Dutch permanent establishment, or to a Dutch legal entity as defined in the General Taxes Act, the VAT is due by the customer (Article 12 VATA 68), so that no VAT is liable by the non-resident entrepreneur (who may not invoice VAT to his or her customer). In this case the customer is liable for VAT at the moment of supply of goods or services.

If the customer is also a non-resident who does not maintain a Dutch permanent establishment or if the customer is a private individual, VAT must be charged and paid to the tax collector by the non-resident supplier.

If the service provider of a business to business supply is not established (and maintains not a permanent establishment) in the Netherlands, and the recipient has a VAT-identification number in the Netherlands, the recipient will be taxed.

(b) Refund of VAT

A non-resident entrepreneur can reclaim the Dutch VAT he or she paid on expenses, investments and importation of goods even if he or she is not involved in taxable transactions in the Netherlands. This refund possibility is in conformity with the EC Directive. The inspector in charge of refunding is the tax office (*Belastingdienst/Ondernemingen buitenland*) in Heerlen.

As of the first of January 2010 it is easier for EU-entrepreneurs to reclaim VAT on foreign supplies. They can reclaim VAT electronically at their own tax authority. Their own tax authority will, if they accept the refund request, send it to the foreign tax authority. The foreign tax authority has to handle the request within the time stipulated.

(c) Fiscal representative

As a result of the completion of the Single Market, foreign entrepreneurs will get more in contact with Dutch VAT. Foreign entrepreneurs are entrepreneurs who are neither established in the Netherlands nor maintain a permanent establishment in the Netherlands.

In general every foreign entrepreneur who performs taxable activities in the Netherlands must be registered. In certain cases the use of a liable fiscal representative is obligatory. There are two systems of fiscal representation.

The fiscal representative with full liability

The fiscal representative with full liability takes care of all Dutch VAT obligations of the foreign entrepreneur, except for import activities (and subsequent deliveries) for which the foreign entrepreneur concerned appointed a representative with limited liability (see below). This way of fiscal representation is obligatory for every entrepreneur who conducts distance sales of over EUR 100,000) to the Netherlands (Article 24d VAT Degree).

The fiscal VAT representative with full liability has to give a bank guarantee to the tax authorities to secure the payment of the VAT due by the foreign entrepreneur and is jointly and severally liable for the amount of tax.

The fiscal representative with limited liability

The fiscal representative with limited liability may only act on behalf of a foreign entrepreneur regarding import and the subsequent deliveries and certain zero-rated supplies. He or she is jointly liable for the amount of tax due and he or she also has to give a bank guarantee to the tax authorities.

8.9 FORMALITIES

In principle, the VAT is paid or deducted through an invoice system; that is, on the basis of invoices issued and received. To the extent that the payment is not received (e.g., in the case of bad debts) the payment and deduction afterwards will be adjusted according to Article 29 VATA 68.

A deduction of VAT is only possible if the VAT has been invoiced in accordance with the legal requirements (Article 35). These invoice requirements are applied very strictly, especially if the seller did not fully account for the VAT.

The VAT must be paid on the basis of a return. The period covered by the return is generally one month. For small amounts, returns may be filed quarterly and, in exceptional cases, annually.

VAT which has not been paid to the tax collector can be additionally assessed. There is a five-year statute of limitation starting at the end of the year to which the additional assessment applies.

In the case of additional VAT assessments or in case of over-payment on the basis of the return filed by the entrepreneur himself or herself, an objection can be filed with the tax authorities. A decision on the basis of this objection is subject to appeal to the Court, eventually to be followed by an appeal to the Court of Appeal and to the Supreme Court.

Finally, it should be noted that the entrepreneur is legally obliged to keep books of 'input' and 'output' on the basis of which the return can be made.

8.10 LISTING

As of the first of January 2010 entrepreneurs who mainly supply services to entrepreneurs established in other Member States of the EU need to record these supplies of services on the internet on a list. This is called listing. The services need to be specified monthly per VAT-identification number of the recipient.

Chapter 9

Estate Tax, Gift Tax

9.1 GENERAL PRINCIPLES

The Estate Tax Act of 1956 (ETA 56) provides for the levy of two taxes:

(a) Estate tax on the value of everything acquired through inheritance from someone who was a resident of the Netherlands at the time of death.
(b) Gift tax on the value of everything acquired by gift from someone who was a resident of the Netherlands at the time of the gift.

The estate tax and gift tax are levied on the acquisition by the heir (donee) regardless of his or her residence. The estate tax is not principally an estate tax in the sense that it taxes the total of the estate, but the rate of tax is based on each share acquired by the respective heir(s), legatee(s) or any other beneficiary through inheritance. The gift tax is, however, calculated on the basis of the total of gifts from one donor to one donee in a calendar year. Gifts made within a period of 180 days before the death are included in the estate for purposes of the estate tax.

Acquisitions subject to a condition precedent will only be taxed once the condition has been fulfilled. Acquisitions subject to a condition subsequent will be taxed at once, but if the condition is fulfilled at a later stage the tax will be adjusted accordingly. The heir (donee) will be taxed as a usufructuary for the period he or she had the usufruct of the gift or the estate.

9.2 RESIDENCE AND NATIONALITY

The taxes discussed in this chapter depend on the residence of the testator or the donor.

The question of where a person is a resident is to be decided on the basis of the actual circumstances (Article 4 GTA, see section 2.1.2).

Individuals in the diplomatic service and their family (household) members outside the Netherlands are always deemed to be resident in the Netherlands.

In principle, nationality is not of importance for the application of ETA 56. There is, however, one important exception. A Netherlands citizen who makes a gift or dies within a period of 10 years after his or her emigration from the Netherlands will be deemed to be a resident of the Netherlands at the time of the gift, or on the date of his or her death. Individuals who are not citizens of the Netherlands will be deemed to be resident in the Netherlands for one year after their emigration for the application of gift tax only.

9.3 GIFTS

For the application of the ETA 56, a gift includes a (formal) gift as defined in the Civil Code (*schenking)* through a notarial deed, or, in the case of movable goods or bearer debts by an (informal) gift (*gift*) as well as any other benefit given without consideration, or a passing of ownership under another legal bases for transfer. If, for example, a house has been sold for a price below market value, which the seller realizes, this can also be considered as a gift. In addition, it also includes any gift which is legally void but nevertheless carried out, and furthermore the payment of any debt or the fulfilment of any obligation which could not legally be claimed is considered a gift. Any advantage from a stipulation or proviso made for the benefit of a third party – unless it is deemed to be a fictitious acquisition through inheritance – is deemed to be a donation by the stipulator to that third party. Furthermore, the designation of goods for the incorporation of a foundation will be deemed to be a gift by the founders to the foundation.

9.4 ACQUISITION THROUGH INHERITANCE

An acquisition through inheritance can result by operation of the inheritance legislation or a last will. In addition to these acquisitions, under ETA 56 a number of acquisitions are deemed to be acquisitions through inheritance.

Two examples are:

- acquisition through a gift made within 180 days before the death of the donor;
- acquisitions through a life insurance contract, provided the premium or any other payment in connection therewith was borne by the policyholder.

9.5 SEPARATED PRIVATE ESTATES

A new system of taxation was introduced as of January 2010 concerning the concept of separated private estates; that is, assets brought into trusts or transferred to foundations. It is of no importance where these foundations are deemed to be resident or under which jurisdiction they were incorporated. For the purpose of inheritance and gift tax (and also income tax) these vehicles will be deemed transparent. The settler is deemed to be the unique holder of the financial interest and will be taxed as if the vehicle would not exist and the assets would remain privately held. Any change of financial interest from the settler to another person will be taxed as a gift from the settler to the new holder of this interest. Upon decease of the settler his or her interest will be taxable with inheritance tax as the heirs will be deemed to have become entitled to the interest. In case the settler might not be able to pay these taxes and the trust or foundation might refuse to do so, the Netherlands Tax Authorities would be entitled to seize property located in the Netherlands, belonging to companies the trust or foundation would hold an interest in.

9.6 VALUATION

The acquisition is valued at the moment it is acquired. In general the tax base will be the 'sales value' (= 'market value').

Shares quoted on the Stock Exchange are valued at the official value, the closing price of the day before.

The sales value for real estate is established at the price which would be paid in the best circumstances by the highest bidder. From 2010 the value for private owned houses will be the value mentioned in the valuation for the real estate tax.

Debt receivables, unquoted shares, etc., are to be valued at their market value. Annuities and the right of usufruct will be valued on the basis of special rates provided for by the estate tax regulations.

A business will be valued on the going concern value or the liquidation value, should the latter be higher.

Special valuation rules apply to land etc. to which the rules of the Estates Act (*Natuur-schoonwet)* 1928 apply (parks, woods, etc.).

For business succession within a family the rate and exemption is very favourable. The first EUR 1,006,000 (2011) is completely tax-exempt and just 17% of the rest (over EUR 1,006,000) of the value of the inherited or given business is taxed, as long as certain conditions are met.

9.7 DEBTS AND FUNERAL EXPENSES

(1) Debts are deductible to the extent they can be legally enforced.
(2) Tax debts are deductible to the extent they relate to events taking place or income received, before the inheritance. Deferred tax liabilities are deductible only in the following cases:
    (a) 30% of the retirements reserve in business assets;
    (b) 20% of other reserves in business assets;
    (c) 30% of the rights to entitlements to periodic payments;

(d) 6.25% of the difference between the value of the shares and their cost price, if these shares form a so-called substantial interest.

(3) Funeral costs are deductible, unless excessive. Expenses related to the settling of the estate are not deductible.

9.8 EXEMPTIONS

There are a large number of exemptions. In this paragraph, only a few will be mentioned.

(a) *Gift tax exemptions:*
- Gifts to the State of the Netherlands; donations to lower public entities if they are in the general interest.
- Gifts to a legal entity, the activities of which are (almost) exclusively in the public interest.
- Gifts from parents to children up to EUR 5,030 (2011). For children between 18–35, a once-only exemption of EUR 26,156 (2011) applies instead of this annual exemption. If a child buys a house the exemption can even be EUR 50,300 (N.B. These amounts are adjusted with an inflation rate correction).
- Gifts which are subject to income tax in the hands of the donee.
- A donation for which the donor can be held to be morally obliged.
- In all other cases EUR 2,012 (2011).

(b) *Estate tax exemptions:*
- Acquisitions by the State or lower public entity if in the public interest.
- Acquisitions by a legal entity, the activities of which are (almost) exclusively in the public interest.
- The first EUR 603,600 (2011) of acquisitions by a spouse or (fiscal) partner.
- The first EUR 19,114 (2011) of acquisitions by children.
- Acquisitions on the basis of a pension scheme.
- The first EUR 19,114 (2011) of acquisitions by grandchildren.
- The first EUR 45,270 (2011) of acquisitions by parents.
- In all other cases, the first EUR 2,012 (2011).

9.9 TAX RATES

For estate, transfer and gift tax the following rates apply:

	I. Spouse, (fiscal) partner and children	I a. Grandchildren	II. Other
0–118,708	10%	18%	30%
118,708 and higher	20%	36%	40%

A person can be a fiscal partner for the gift and inheritance tax if he or she was or is married, is a registered partner or has a notarial cohabitation contract. In the latter case, the two persons will also have to have lived at the same address for six months (estate tax) or two years (gift tax), and not be related in the direct line. If two adult persons not being related in the direct line live at the same address for more than five years, they will be treated as partners also, even if they have not entered into a notarial cohabitation contract.

Chapter 10

Transfer Tax, Insurance Tax

10.1 INTRODUCTION

The Legal Transactions Act (*Wet op belastingen rechtsverkeer*) of 24 December 1970 introduced some indirect taxes. These taxes are:

(1) Transfer tax
(2) Insurance tax

10.2 TRANSFER TAX

10.2.1 Tax upon Transfer of Real Estate

The tax is levied upon the acquisition of real estate, situated in the Netherlands, and upon the acquisition of certain rights related to immovable property.

10.2.2 Taxable Event

The taxable event is the acquisition of the legal and the beneficial ownership (title) to the property, not the contract to buy immovable property. Consequently, the tax is levied upon delivery of the immovable property which is effected by a notarial deed.

10.2.3 Taxable Base

The taxable base is the fair market value of the immovable property on the date of delivery. With respect to transactions between unrelated parties, this value will normally be equal to the sales price. If, however, the price is higher (or lower) than the fair market value, the tax is levied on the higher of sales price or market value.

10.2.4 Tax Rate

The tax is collected from the buyer. The rate is 6%. The notary before whom the deed is passed charges the tax to the buyer and pays it to the tax authorities.

10.2.5 Real Property Rights

In the case of rights to real property (e.g., leasehold) the taxable base is also the value of the right. In the case of acquisition of a leasehold the value of the right is increased by the discounted value of the expected future lease payments. The taxable base does not, however, exceed the present market value of the property. No transfer tax is levied upon the acquisition of certain immovable rights, including mortgages.

10.2.6 Transfer of Economic Property

According to the present law, the acquisition of economic ownership of real estate is a taxable event. Thus it is possible for a seller and a buyer to agree that, from a certain date, immovable property will be for the account and risk of the buyer without transferring the title. In that case the tax is levied at the moment the buyer acquires the economic ownership.

10.2.7 Other Acquisitions

Apart from the acquisition of real estate, taxable events are:

(a) the acquisition of shares in a real estate company where the direct or indirect interest of the acquirer, together with that of his or her partner, in the company after the acquisition exceeds 7% of the share capital, and his or her interest, together with that of his or her nearest relatives, is at least 1/3 of the share capital;
(b) the acquisition of certain certificates entitling the holder to a pro rata share of immovable property; and
(c) the acquisition of a membership in an association, if that membership entitles the member to make use of immovable property (e.g., an association owning residential property on behalf of its members).

10.2.8 TAXABLE BASE AND PAYMENT OF TAX

The acquisition of shares, certificates and memberships referred to in section 10.2.7 is taxed as acquisitions of real estate. The taxable base is, however, the pro rata part of the value of the underlying property, not the price paid for the shares, etc. The acquisition of shares etc. does not require the participation of a notary public. Consequently the tax has to be paid by the buyer within one month after the acquisition.

10.2.9 NON-ACQUISITION

A number of acquisitions are not considered as acquisitions for transfer tax purposes, e.g., acquisition by inheritance, by marriage, by division of an estate amongst the heirs, and by accession.

10.2.10 TRANSFER WITHIN SIX MONTHS

In the case of transfer of a property within six months after a transfer of the same property (including a transfer through shares, etc., as indicated in section 10.2.7) the tax is reduced by the tax due upon the previous transfer (e.g., transfer in January at 100, transfer in May of the same year at 110: transfer tax on the second transfer 6% of 10).

10.2.11 OTHER EXEMPTIONS

Provided that the notary (or the buyer) claims the exemption in the tax return, the transfer is exempt in various cases; the most important are:

(a) transfer of immovable property if VAT is due on the same transfer (for constructed real estate until two years after the first use) unless the property has been used as a business asset and the transferee may (partially or completely) deduct the VAT;
(b) transfer of an enterprise including immovable property to the transferor's children who continue that enterprise;
(c) acquisitions by public bodies;
(d) transfer to a partnership, and transfer to a company in exchange for shares, if the immovable property belongs to an enterprise which is completely transferred to that partnership or company;
(e) upon liquidation of partnerships, etc., provided that the immovable property is transferred to the partner who transferred the property to the partnership, or his or her heirs. The exemption depends of earlier transfers, if they were tax-exempt or not;

(f) in certain cases, if property is transferred within a group of companies ('internal reorganizations'); and
(g) in the case of the acquisition of property by the person who constructed a building. (E.g., A built a house on the land of B. Upon the transfer of land and building by B to A the tax is levied on the value (price) of the land only.)

10.3 INSURANCE TAX

10.3.1 Taxable Event

Insurance tax is due if the insured risk is situated within the Netherlands. The insured risk is situated within the Netherlands, if:

(a) the holder of the insurance policy is resident within the Netherlands; or
(b) if the holder of the policy is a legal entity, to which the insurance relates, and that entity is resident in the Netherlands.

The insured risk is in some cases deemed to be in the Netherlands, for example, if the insurance policy covers real estate in the Netherlands or motor cars, ships and aircrafts registered within the Netherlands.

10.3.2 Taxable Base and Tax Rate

The taxable base is the insurance premium. The rate is 9.7%.

The insurance company or its representative in the Netherlands has to pay the tax to the tax authorities and charges the tax to the insured person. If the policy is not issued by a company or representative in the Netherlands the insured person must pay the tax himself or herself. The tax is levied on the premium.

10.3.3 Exemptions

Certain types of insurances are exempt, such as:

- life insurance;
- accident insurance;
- invalidity and disability insurance;
- medical expenses and health insurance;
- unemployment insurance;
- insurance of sea-going vessels (with the exception of yachts);
- insurance of international aircrafts;
- transportation insurance;
- reinsurance; and
- credit insurance in respect of export transactions.

Chapter 11
International and European Tax Law

11.1 GENERAL

National states generally found their right to tax on the principle of residence, the principle of source and often also the principle of nationality. A state may thus have created taxation rights in its domestic law, but this does not imply that it will under all circumstances be allowed to make use of these taxation rights. These rights may be limited by international tax law (unilateral rules and Double Taxation Conventions) and European tax law. Besides posing limitations on taxation rights of states, both international and European tax law contain measures developed to prevent tax avoidance. Moreover, both Double Taxation Conventions (hereafter referred to as tax treaties) and European tax law contain rules preventing discrimination, as well as rules regarding the exchange of information between tax administrations and the assistance in the recovery of tax claims. This chapter contains a short overview of the international tax law and European tax law applicable in the Netherlands.

11.2 UNILATERAL RELIEF: THE DEGREE FOR THE AVOIDANCE OF DOUBLE TAXATION 2001

The Decree for the Avoidance of Double Taxation 2001 (*Besluit voorkoming dubbele belasting* 2001) basically fulfils two functions:

(i) it provides for unilateral rules for domestic taxpayers in the Netherlands preventing double taxation for the following taxes: income tax, wage tax, corporate income tax, estate tax, gift tax and gaming tax. Two instruments are available for this purpose: exemption and credit (see further section 11.4.1).

(ii) the Decree also has a normative function: treaties refer to the Decree for further details on the application of the exemption and the credit method, being also the methods used to prevent double taxation for tax treaty purposes.

The Decree is only applicable insofar as no other provision for the prevention of double taxation is applicable. Thus the Decree is applicable if:

- there is no treaty;
- there is a treaty, but this treaty is not applicable for certain taxes and these taxes are within the scope of the Decree;
- there is a treaty, but this treaty does not contain a rule in respect of a specific taxpayer or taxable object.

The Decree only prevents juridical double taxation. Juridical double taxation occurs if one taxable subject is taxed twice on his or her taxable income by two or more tax administrations. An example is a taxpayer who resides in the Netherlands and works in Germany. The Netherlands taxes the person on his or her worldwide income because he or she is a resident in the Netherlands. Germany taxes the person on his or her income from labour because the source of the income is in Germany.

The Decree does not prevent economical double taxation, which occurs if two taxable subjects are taxed on the same income by one or more tax administrations. Economical double taxation occurs for instance if a shareholder receives dividend on his or her shares in a company. The profits of the company are taxed with corporate income tax and the shareholder is taxed with personal income tax.

The Decree provides only to some extent for rules concerning the avoidance of double taxation. And in respect of dividends important rule is the 'beneficial ownership' rule providing that no credit will be provided if the person who formally receives a dividend is a conduit for another person and the latter person is to a lesser extent eligible for a reduction of tax due in the Netherlands than the person receiving the dividend in the first instance.

11.3 TAX TREATIES

11.3.1 General

Double tax agreements allocate taxation rights. They either grant:

- the country of residence the sole right to tax the income;
- the country of source the right to tax the income, while maintaining the right for the country of residence to take into account progressive effects of income taxes by providing 'exemption with progression';
- the country of source the right to levy a low withholding tax while the country of residence has the right to include the income in worldwide income, under the condition that this country will also provide for a tax credit.

Most tax treaties are based on either Model Tax Treaties published by the OECD[1] or by the United Nations.

Besides allocating taxation rights tax treaties also contain provisions to prevent avoidance of taxation, such as:

- a beneficial ownership clause in respect of withholding taxes on dividend, interest and royalties;[2]
- look through approaches disallowing treaty benefits to a company not owned, directly or indirectly, by residents of the State of which the company is a resident;
- clauses granting treaty benefits only in case the income derived from the source state is taxed in the state of residence according to the ordinary rules of that state;
- channel approach provisions disallowing treaty benefits in case the income is used to satisfy claims by persons not resident of the Contracting State;
- exclusion approaches excluding certain entities from treaty benefits.

Moreover tax treaties contain rules:

- making exchange of information possible for the competent authorities of the Contracting States, either on request, automatically or spontaneously;
- providing comprehensive assistance in the collection of taxes.

Tax treaties also contain rules to prevent discrimination. Article 24(1) OECD forbids discrimination on ground of nationality. Subject to reciprocity, the nationals of a Contracting State may not be less favourably treated in the other Contracting State than nationals of that other State in the same circumstances. Article 24(2) OECD provides for equal treatment with nationals of a Contracting State solely to stateless persons who are residents of that or of the other Contracting State. Article 24(3) rules that the taxation of a permanent establishment shall not be less favourably levied in the State concerned than the taxation levied on enterprises of that State carrying on the same activities, and thus focuses on residency instead of nationality. Article 24(4) OECD provides that interest, royalties and other disbursements paid by an enterprise of a Contracting State to a resident of the other Contracting State shall be deductible under the same conditions as if they had been paid to a resident of the first-mentioned State for the purpose of determining the taxable profits of such enterprise. Article 25(5) OECD forbids a Contracting State to give less favourable treatment to an enterprise, the capital of which is owned or controlled, wholly or partly, directly or indirectly, by one or more residents of the other Contracting State.

Finally tax treaties provide for mutual agreement. The mutual agreement procedure may be invoked by the taxpayer in case of taxation not in accordance

1. The OECD published Model Tax Conventions in 1963, 1977, 1992, 2005 and 2010. The United Nations published Model Tax Conventions in 1980 and 2001.
2. The Netherlands levies a withholding tax on dividend only. Other states generally also levy a withholding tax on interest and royalties.

with the provisions of the treaty. There are no sanctions if the tax authorities do not come to a mutual agreement. Therefore, the OECD included the possibility of arbitration in the Model Treaty in 2008.

The competent authorities may also invoke a mutual agreement procedure in case of any difficulties or doubts arising as to the interpretation or application of the treaty or for the elimination of double taxation in cases not provided for in the treaty.

With the exception of the non-discrimination benefits, treaty benefits are granted to residents of Contracting States. The term 'residency' is further explained in Article 4 of the treaty. Often the Article 4 OECD provision has been included in the bilateral tax treaty: for the purposes of the treaty (not for applying domestic rules!) the term resident of a Contracting State means any person who, under the laws of that State, is liable to tax therein by reason of his or her domicile, residence, place of management or any other criterion of a similar nature. Tax treaties contain tie-breaker rules in order to solve situations where a taxpayer under domestic provisions is liable to tax in two countries. For individuals the following criteria are decisive: permanent home, centre of vital interest, habitual abode, nationality, mutual agreement. For companies the place of effective management is decisive.

11.3.2 Tax Treaties Concluded by the Netherlands

11.3.2.1 Extensive Treaty Network

The Netherlands has concluded an extensive network of double tax treaties of – at the time of writing (April 2011) about 90 tax treaties covering income tax, withholding tax and often also wealth tax. Moreover, the Netherlands has concluded eight treaties covering estate tax and gift tax. Tax treaties concluded by the Netherlands in the 1960s, 1970s and early 1980s with OECD-Member States generally resemble the OECD Model (1963 or 1977). Most treaties concluded in the late eighties and nineties resemble the Netherlands Standard Tax Treaty that the Netherlands published in 1987.

This Standard Treaty to a great extent resembles the OECD-Model but contains some important deviations such as rules concerning redemption of pensions and life insurance policies, a 0% rate for participation dividends and interest, and a provision allowing the Netherlands to levy according to its own law an exit tax on gains from the alienation of shares being part of a substantial shareholding in the course of – in older treaties – five or – in newer treaties – ten years after emigration. In most double tax agreements also other deviations occur as the contracting states want to take into account their specific economic circumstances and legislation.

Moreover, the Secretary of State for Finance published a Memorandum on Dutch Tax Policy in 1998. A revised Memorandum is expected in 2011.

11.3.2.2 Structure of Tax Treaties Concluded by the Netherlands

Generally tax treaties concluded by the Netherlands have the following structure (which is similar to that of the OECD and the UN model):

- Chapter I Scope of the treaty
  - Article 1 Persons covered
  - Article 2 Taxes covered
- Chapter II Definitions
  - Article 3 General definitions
  - Article 4 Residents
  - Article 5 Permanent establishment
- Chapter III Taxation of income
  - Article 6 Income from immovable property
  - Article 7 Business profits
  - Article 8 Shipping, inland waterways transport and air transport
  - Article 9 Associated enterprises
  - Article 10 Dividends
  - Article 11 Interest
  - Article 12 Royalties
  - Article 13 Capital gains
  - Article 14 Independent personal services (deleted as from 2000)
  - Article 15 Income from employment
  - Article 16 Director's fees
  - Article 17 Artistes and sportsmen
  - Article 18 Pensions
  - Article 19 Government services
  - Article 20 Students
  - Article 21 Other income
- Chapter IV Taxation of capital
  - Article 22 Capital
- Chapter V Methods for elimination of double taxation
  - Article 23 A Exemption method
  - Article 23 B Credit method
- Chapter VI Special provisions
  - Article 24 Non-discrimination
  - Article 25 Mutual Agreement Procedure
  - Article 26 Exchange of information
- Chapter VII Final provisions
  - Article 27 Members of Diplomatic missions and consular posts
  - Article 28 Territorial extension
  - Article 29 Entry into force
  - Article 30 Termination
- Terminal clause
- Protocol

In general the source state is allowed to tax income from immovable property.

Allocation rights on active income, business profits and income from employment are allocated to the state of source provided a certain threshold is passed. In respect of business profits a permanent establishment should be present in the source state. In respect of income from employment either the employee should be present for more than 183 days in the source state or the remuneration should be paid by, or on behalf of, an employer who is a resident of the source state, or the remuneration is borne by a permanent establishment of the employer in the source state. The state of residence should provide for relief of double taxation.

Alternative provisions are available for:

- shipping, inland waterways and air transport (in most treaties this income shall be taxable only in the contracting state in which the place of effective management is situated);
- directors fees (in most treaties this income may be taxed in the contracting state of which the company is a resident); and
- students' income (in most treaties this income shall not be taxed in the visiting state provided the payments arise from sources outside that state).

Many treaties concluded by the Netherlands moreover contain a provision for professors and other teachers (in most treaties the income will be taxable in the state of residence provided the professor or teacher does not teach or do research at a university in another country for a period of more than two years).

Income derived from government services generally is taxable only in the state paying the salary, wage or similar remuneration. However, the state of residence is allowed to tax these remunerations if the taxpayer is a national of that state and did not become a resident of that state solely for the purpose of rendering the services.

Treaties reading similar to the OECD-Model allocate taxation rights on pension payments and annuities to the state of residence. The OECD, however, mentions source taxation as alternative. In approximately one-third of the treaties concluded by the Netherlands,[3] especially the newer ones, source taxation on periodical pension payments is the general rule. This may be in the form of:

- general source taxation;
- limited source state taxation: the source state may tax pension and annuity payments but the tax is limited to a certain amount;
- provisional source state taxation: the Netherlands may apply source state taxation on pensions and annuities as long as this income is tax-exempt in the other state;
- residence taxation with adequate taxation clause providing that the source state taxes at least 90% of the gross amount of the payments at the rate generally applicable to income from employment income.

Moreover, as of the late seventies of the previous century, most tax treaties concluded by the Netherlands contain a provision allocating a taxing right on lump

3. A country exempting pension rights and taxing the pension payments and annuities.

sum payments upon redemption of pension rights and annuities to the source state as anti-avoidance rule.

Taxation rights on passive income (dividend, interest, labour) are allocated to both the state of residence and the state of source. The source state however should reduce the tax rate taken into account. The OECD-Model advises:

- for dividend a rate of 5% (in case the dividend is received by a company owning 25% or more of the shares) and 15% for dividends (in all other cases);
- for interest a rate of 10%.

If the right to tax is allocated to the source state the state of residence should prevent double taxation. The OECD advises to tax royalties only in the country of residence of the beneficial owner. The Netherlands tax treaties generally contain the following rates:

- for dividends: explicit tax policy is that the Netherlands strives for a rate of 0% in case the beneficial owner is a company which holds directly at least 25% of the capital of the company paying the dividends; there is no explicit policy for other cases;
- for interest and royalties: explicit tax policy is that the Netherlands strives for a rate of 0%.

11.3.2.3 Interpretation Issues

The Commentary to the OECD-Model, which is part of the context of bilateral treaties, is used for interpretation purposes. The Netherlands adheres to the dynamic approach with respect to treaty interpretation as laid down in this Commentary. Changes or additions to the Commentary should be taken into account in interpreting and applying a bilateral tax treaty if the provisions of the treaty are similar in substance to the articles in the OECD Model.

11.4 METHODS FOR ELIMINATING DOUBLE TAXATION USED BY THE NETHERLANDS

11.4.1 Exemption or Credit

The OECD-Model and UN-Model provide for either exemption or credit as methods to prevent double taxation. The OECD and the UN leave the choice which of these methods will be used for which type of income to the contracting states.

In the Commentary to the OECD-Model two types of exemption provisions and two types of credit provisions are described:

(a) full exemption
(b) exemption with progression

(c) full credit
(d) ordinary credit.

In view of the wide variety of fiscal policies and techniques applied by their Member States in respect of the calculation of the exemption and the credit, the OECD and the UN do not provide detailed rules.

The Netherlands Decree for the avoidance of double taxation as referred to in section 11.2 uses both the exemption and the credit method. Tax treaties concluded by the Netherlands since 1980 refer to this Decree for the technique of determining the amount of the exemption or credit. The Decree, several administrative decrees and case law concerning this Decree deal with issues such as costs to be attributed to foreign-source income, personal deductions, per country or overall exemption or credit, carry-forward of unused foreign income and excess credits.

Below the exemption method and the credit method will be explained in more detail for the income tax and corporate income tax, as well as for the estate tax and the gift tax.

11.4.2 Income Tax and Corporate Income Tax

11.4.2.1 Full Exemption

In case a treaty provision concluded by the Netherlands uses the wording 'shall be taxable only' full exemption will be provided. Generally it is the state of source that has to give up its taxation rights. In tax treaties concluded by the Netherlands this is often the case in respect of profits from the operation of ships or aircraft in international traffic, pension income, interest and royalties. The income derived in the source state is not included in the taxable base in the state of residence.

11.4.2.2 Exemption with Progression

Exemption with progression generally is applicable for income from immovable property, business profits and income from employment. The wording used in the tax treaty is 'may be taxed' in the source state. The exemption with progression method taxes domestic income at the rate which would have been applied if the worldwide income would be fully taxable in the Netherlands. Thus including foreign-source income in worldwide income, but only for purposes of the applicable tax rate.

Though exemption with progression is an exemption method, the Netherlands while calculating the exemption with progression uses the same formula as is used to calculate the ordinary credit that is part of the credit method. The formula that is used to calculate the exemption with progression is the pro rata tax that will be deducted from the tax on worldwide income:

$$\frac{\textit{foreign income} \times \text{tax on worldwide income}}{\text{worldwide income}}$$

The difference with the ordinary credit method is that in case of exemption with progression the calculated amount is the amount that will be deducted from the tax on worldwide income, whereas in the case of ordinary credit it is the maximum amount that will be deducted. That is: if the ordinary credit method is applied the foreign tax will be deducted from the tax on worldwide income unless the amount calculated by using the formula above is lower.

In other states exemption with progression often only implies that the tax rate that would be applicable on worldwide income is applied on domestic income. The difference between this method and the method applied in the Netherlands described above is that foreign losses are taken into account when using the method applied in the Netherlands and are not taken into account when the other method is used.

11.4.2.3 Full Credit

In case a full credit is provided the tax paid abroad by the taxpayer is deducted from the domestic tax due on his or her worldwide income. Resident states are not prepared to grant full credit as this would imply that more credit has to be given by the state of residence than the tax that is related in the state of residence to the income derived in the state of source.

11.4.2.4 Ordinary Credit

Countries are prepared to grant an ordinary credit. This limits the deduction of foreign tax to the amount of tax which would have been due on the foreign part of the income if it were taxed domestically. In tax treaties concluded by the Netherlands generally such credit is provided for dividend, interest and royalty income and often also for income derived by artists and sporters.

11.4.3 Estate Tax and Gift Tax

With respect to the estate tax relief the Unilateral Decree for the Avoidance of Double Taxation provides for the credit method for business assets and immovable properties provided that they are subject to an estate tax abroad. The amount of the relief is equal to the lower of the estate tax levied abroad or the estate tax levied due over the assets in the Netherlands:

$$\frac{\textit{Qualifying assets} \times \text{Netherlands estate tax due}}{\text{Total assets}}$$

For calculation of the numerator of the fraction, the debts of a foreign permanent establishment and debts secured by mortgage on real estate as well as the exemptions may be deducted.

A Netherlands citizen who emigrated from the Netherlands is deemed to be a resident of the Netherlands due to the provisions mentioned in section 2.1.2.

For this citizen, relief from double taxation can be obtained in the same manner and for the same assets as described above. Furthermore, in that case avoidance of double taxation can be obtained with respect to other assets over which estate tax is due abroad, which would not have been due if the deceased would in fact have been a resident of the Netherlands. Such with the exception of assets of a domestic business or a participation therein otherwise than as a shareholder; real property situated in the Netherlands and profit-sharing rights not derived from shares or through an employment.

For the calculation of the Netherlands estate tax the foreign estate tax due can be credited against the value of the assets in case of an inheritance from a resident of the Netherlands of assets located abroad which would not qualify for the relief of double taxation as described above. The same rules apply with respect to the gift tax.

As mentioned above the Netherlands has concluded eight tax treaties covering estate tax, with the following countries: Austria, Belgium, Finland, Israel, Sweden, Switzerland and the United States of America. The treaties with Belgium and the United Kingdom and Northern Ireland also contain provision to prevent double gift tax.

11.5 EUROPEAN TAX LAW

11.5.1 Direct Taxes

11.5.1.1 Rules Limiting Taxation Rights in Domestic Tax Law

Taxation rights created in domestic law may also be limited by European tax law. As tax treaties only prevent juridical double taxation and there are blind spots in the treaty network between the Member States, rules have been developed on a European level to prevent economical double taxation.

These rules are:

- the Parent-subsidiary Directive 90/435/EG as amended by Directive 2003/123/EC;
- the Merger Directive 2009/133/EG;
- and the Interest-Royalty Directive 2003/49/EC as amended by Directive 2004/76/EC.

Directives must be implemented in the domestic legislation of the Member States. The changes required in the Dutch domestic tax law were relatively limited as the existing legislation contained similar rules.

The Parent-Subsidiary Directive provides for relief of double corporate income tax within a group of companies having their residence both for domestic tax law and tax treaties in the Member States. The state of residence of the parent company should provide for exemption or credit. The Netherlands corporate income tax law provides for the participation exemption. The Directive also provides for relief of dividend withholding tax within a group of companies having their residence both for domestic tax law and tax treaties in the Member States. The Netherlands extended the scope of the exemption in the Dividend Tax Act 1965 to dividends paid to parent companies being resident in an EU Member State.

The Merger Directive provides for deferral of personal income tax and corporate income tax in case of exchange of shares, transfer of assets, legal mergers and divisions. The scope of the exchange of shares facility and the transfer of assets facility in the Dutch income tax act and corporate income tax act were amended accordingly.

The Interest-Royalty Directive provides for relief of double taxation on interest and royalties within a group of companies. As the Netherlands did not levy a withholding tax on interest and royalties at the time the Directive was adopted, no amendments were necessary.

11.5.1.2 Arbitration

Arbitration in tax cases is provided for by EU-legislation, although not in the form of a Directive. The Member States signed an Arbitration Convention, as they wanted a Committee of tax experts instead of the EC Court of Justice to deal with the matter. The scope is restricted to transfer pricing cases, whereas the taxpayer may request arbitration for any issue not resolved by mutual agreement. The Netherlands signed the Arbitration Convention.

11.5.1.3 Non-discrimination

EU-legislation does not provide for specific rules disallowing discrimination in the field of direct taxation. However, the general non-discrimination rules provided for in the EU treaty also apply to direct tax cases. These rules are:

- Article 18 Treaty on the Functioning of European Union (TFEU)[4] (= Article 12 EC[5]) prohibiting discrimination on grounds of nationality;
- Article 45 TFEU (= Article 39 EC) safeguarding the free movement of persons within the EC;
- Article 49 TFEU (= Article 43 EC) safeguarding the freedom of establishment;
- Article 56 TFEU (= Article 49 EC) safeguarding freedom of providing services within the EC;
- Article 65 EC safeguarding freedom of capital movements.

Neither domestic legislation, nor international tax treaties may contain discriminative rules. Case law showed that Netherlands income tax and corporate income tax contained some discriminative elements. They were amended accordingly. One of the famous cases of the EC Court of Justice concerning Dutch tax legislation is

4. Treaty for the Functioning of the European Union in force as from 1 Dec. 2009.
5. The EC-Treaty in force up to 1 Dec. 2009.

the Bosal case, European Court of Justice (ECJ) 18 September 2003, C-18/01. Article 13 CITA 69 at the time disallowed deduction of costs that did not directly have a relation with profits that would be derived in the Netherlands. Bosal Holding BV, resident of the Netherlands, thus could not claim tax relief for interest paid on borrowing financing subsidiaries which did not generate income taxable in the Netherlands. The ECJ considered this provision contradictory to Article 43 EC. The Netherlands amended its legislation accordingly.

11.5.2 Indirect Taxes

11.5.2.1 Unification

The EU is a customs union. Therefore, rules on customs duties have been unified since the treaty of Rome was concluded in 1957.

11.5.2.2 Harmonization

Sales taxes have been harmonized in the EU since 1967. In that year with the French value added tax system as example the First VAT-Directive was adopted. Due to this Directive a common system was introduced. After that First Directive some twenty other VAT-Directives have been adopted. In 2006 all these VAT-Directives have been replaced by one comprehensive Directive. The Netherlands implemented these Directives in its legislation.

In respect of excises less harmonization took place. Common rules have been developed for alcoholic beverages, manufactured tobacco products and energy products. These Directives also have been implemented in the Dutch tax legislation.

Moreover, in 2003, an energy tax directive has been adopted setting a minimum excise duty for oil products, gas, electricity and coals. This Directive has been implemented in the Dutch tax legislation as well.

11.5.2.3 Non-discrimination

Specific rules concerning non-discrimination in the field of indirect taxes have been part of treaties concerning the EEC/EC and EU since 1957. Articles 28–30 TFEU (Articles 23–25 EC) guarantees free movements of goods. Article 110 TFEU (Article 90 EC) prohibits discriminatory and protective internal taxes.

Chapter 12
Miscellaneous

12.1 REAL PROPERTY TAX

As already mentioned in the introduction (Chapter 1) local authorities may levy certain taxes. The most important is the real estate tax. This tax is based on the ownership of the property. The Act providing for the right of the municipalities to levy a real estate tax recognizes only one system: the tax has to be based on the value of the property. There are exemptions, for example, for churches, certain estates, etc.

12.2 IMPORT DUTIES

The Netherlands is part of the customs area of the EU.

The import duties are levied on the basis of EU regulations. Import duties are levied if goods are imported from non-EU countries. In addition, the EU has entered into international agreements which allow the import of goods or certain goods from certain countries at a lower or sometimes even zero rate.

Import duties, which are the same for the whole of the EU, are generally levied as a percentage of the import value. The percentages have been provided for in the tariff of import duties. The import value is established in accordance with the customs valuation code of the GATT.

Furthermore, the customs regulations provide for certain exemptions for which, generally, a permit is required (e.g., removal of household furniture, transport vehicles temporarily imported, etc.). A number of exemptions also apply to the levy of VAT and excise duty at importation.

If goods have been imported and the import duty has been paid, a refund of import duty will only be possible in a very limited number of cases, for example, goods returned because of defects. Goods imported can be stored in a bonded warehouse (*entrepot*) in order to defer the payment of import duty, or to prevent payment in those cases where the goods are ultimately destined for non-EU countries.

12.3 AGRICULTURAL LEVIES

In order to control the market for agricultural goods in the EU, various agricultural regulations provide for levies and subsidies in the case of import of certain agricultural products, and levies and refunds in the case of export.

12.4 EXCISE TAXES

A one-time excise tax is levied upon the importation of certain goods. In the Netherlands the following goods are subject to excise tax:

- beer;
- alcohol and products containing alcohol;
- wine;
- sugar;
- tobacco imports;
- mineral oils;
- certain non-alcoholic drinks.

12.5 LOTTERY TAX

A withholding tax of 29% is withheld on prizes exceeding EUR 454 (2011) derived from games of chance. If there can be assigned market value to a good, it will be taxed for that value as price.

12.6 MOTOR VEHICLE TAX

This is a tax levied on the owner of a motor vehicle.

Appendix

The Graded Tax System of the Income Tax

		Income Tax/National Insurance Contributions (%)
Younger than 65 years; born in 1946		
1	€ 0 up to and including € 18,628	33.00
2	€ 18,629 up to and including € 33,436	41.95
3	€ 33,437 up to and including € 55,694	42.00
4	€ 55,695 Or more	52.00
65 years and older; born in 1945 or earlier		
1	€ 0 up to and including € 18,628	15.10
2	€ 18,629 up to and including € 33,485	24.05
3	€ 33,486 up to and including € 55,694	42.00
4	€ 55,695 or more	52.00